INK

INK

The Years of Journalism
Before the Days of Bloggers

a memoir

Robert Coram

I N K
The Years of Journalism
Before the Days of Bloggers

Cover Design by Jason Orr
Author Photo by Jeff Von Hoene

ISBN: 978-0-9983820-3-6

Published by:
Five Bridges Press
Atlanta, GA USA

For JFA

I owe you everything

Safe journey

The only things that are important in life are the things you remember.

—Jean Renoir

1

One day in February 1961, I entered an Atlanta lobby to interview for the job I had wanted since I was a teenager: reporter at the most prominent newspaper in the South. I was twenty-four, had flunked out of college, served three sentences in a military stockade—which, if you want to get technical, can be called a federal penitentiary— been tossed out of the US Air Force, served a year on probation for letting a patient escape from a mental institution, and then come to Atlanta, where I had been fired from my first three jobs.

One stupid mistake after another. But life had given me more chances than most. I counted them. The interview at the paper was my tenth chance, and I had to make it work. I had to begin the work I was meant to do.

I had returned to college and was a sophomore who was about to interview with a great newspaper at a time when Atlanta was about to become the center of the biggest story in America—the civil rights movement.

When I entered the lobby, I stepped onto a tight rope stretching across an abyss. On the far side was redemption, the chance to break the chain of failures that was my life. I could fulfill my dream of becoming a newspaper reporter. But in between was a city editor who, if he learned of my past, would end the interview, and I would be an example of how a few bad decisions can ruin a young man's life.

My daddy had been a career army sergeant, and he had pounded honesty and character and integrity into me. A thousand times, he'd said, "Your reputation is all you got, boy. Nobody can take it away from you. Only you can give it away."

I had given my reputation away. I wanted it back.

This interview was a chance that would come only once. And I knew if the city editor asked about my background, I would lie. And the lying would be a continuation of my failures. Thinking of the job as a chance for redemption was bullshit logic.

I took several hesitant steps and stopped in the middle of the brown marble floor, transfixed, and turned in a slow circle as I took in everything, soaking up the look and the feel and the sounds of this legendary newspaper. This was where publisher Ralph McGill thundered out his editorials as he led the South toward enlightenment. This was where John Pennington and Jack Nelson, two great investigative reporters, put the fear of God into malefactors and public officials and anyone else who strayed from the course of righteousness. When a white staff car of this newspaper rolled outside the city limits, people stopped and stared. Wherever the car stopped, some poor bastard was about to have his ass handed to him.

I was in a holy place. And for me, it was the right place.

When I was growing up in a small southwest Georgia town, my mornings were cut from an unchanging pattern: the sound of Daddy's boots as he tromped through the bedroom, the smell of coffee and biscuits as Mother prepared breakfast, and the faint rustle as Daddy opened the *Atlanta Constitution*. Silence. I waited. Then came a burst of profanity, and I knew Daddy was reading Ralph McGill's column. Daddy disagreed with just about everything McGill wrote. But still, he read the column. I figured that any man who could so consistently generate such anger in my daddy was someone I wanted to emulate.

The first faint rumblings of wanting to be a newspaperman fit into a pattern I would not see for years: those who escape from a small Southern town often find their life's work in a field far removed, even unknown, in that small town. No one from my hometown had ever been a writer. I wanted to move as far as possible from my hometown and to be everything I could never be if I stayed. I wanted to be a newspaperman in Atlanta.

Now I was in the lobby of the Atlanta newspapers.

Under my feet, I felt a faint quiver that turned into a deep and sustained seismic rumble. The presses were running. The great insatiable news beast was gnashing its teeth and today would spit out a quarter of a million copies of the *Journal*. Whether the paper landed on doorsteps of ordinary citizens or the desks of high public officials, it would be handled with reverence and read with intensity. Humiliation, jail sentences, public careers, and eternal glory were found within these pages.

Here, the two Atlanta papers, the *Atlanta Journal* and the *Atlanta Constitution*, were published. Because of McGill, I had dreamed of working for the *Constitution*. But I was interviewing with the *Journal*, and that was fine by me. I stepped aboard the elevator and saw the *Journal* was on the fourth floor. I pressed the button. When the doors opened, I paused, stepped out, paused again. I could *feel* the spirits of the reporters and editors and photographers who had been here before. Just as one can feel the spirit of Tom Paine in Valley Forge, or Matthew Brady at Gettysburg, or Floyd Gibbons at Belleau Wood, or Ernie Pyle on Ryukyu. So I could feel the spirits of my professional antecedents. To you, this may sound like romantic nonsense. But newspaper people understand. That is, old-time newspaper people.

I turned right and, a few steps later, was facing a long hall that ended in the sprawling cacophonous beehive that was the city room. Under my feet, I still felt the rumbling of the beast that had to be fed many times a day. The news beast would eat the ambitious and spit out the weak and trample the doubtful. Only those born to the ink would survive.

I walked at a slow pace down the hall.

The sports department was on the right. Through the open door, I saw men leaning over typewriters, typing with great intensity, studying sheets of paper as they hurried from desk to desk. I recognized Furman Bisher, one of the most famous sportswriters in America, who directed one of the best sports departments in America. Across the hall was the women's department, where elegant and smartly dressed women glided about and smiled tight superior smiles without cracking their makeup.

The hall opened into the large city room. Rows and rows of desk with reporters hammering away at their typewriters. A reporter looked up, held several pages of paper aloft, and screamed, "Copy!" in a voice that could have been heard a block away. A wiry teenager ran to the reporter's desk, grabbed the sheets of paper, and rushed them to the city desk. The reporter stuck the yellow carbon copies of the story on a pencil-thin spike atop his desk. Occasionally, a reporter raised his eyes from his typewriter and shouted a question to the room at large. An answer was shouted back, and the reporter, eyes still focused on his typewriter, elbows splayed, resumed typing.

Several dozen typewriters being pounded, people shouting, and the high-pitched chatter of a half-dozen teletype machines against the wall all combined to make the room a deafening industrial place—a place where the truth was hammered out. No one seemed to notice the noise. And even though there was a feeling of urgency, everyone moved with a sure sense of purpose.

The city desk was straight ahead, and every activity in the newsroom was focused around the man at that desk: the city editor. He was a heavy, grim-faced man who would accept a sheet of paper from a copy boy, bend over it with a thick-leaded pencil and blank out words, make paragraph marks, and fling the paper to one of the men sitting in front of him. He did so in a quick and assured manner, little thought, lots of experience. The man to whom he flung the paper made more marks, shouted, "Copy!" and a copy boy grabbed the paper and rushed it to the copy desk, a large U-shaped desk with a small, gnomish man sitting at the center and three copy editors down each side. I knew it was the copy desk because I saw my journalism professor bent over a piece of paper but did not want to call out to her.

The beefy man at the city desk looked up, impatient eyes boring into me.

"I'm here to see the city editor," I said. "My name is Robert Coram."

He stuck out his hand and said he was the city editor and his name was Harold Davis. He pointed to a row of chairs and said, "Have a seat over there. Give me a couple of minutes. We are pushing a deadline."

I sat. Not a single curious glance came my way. But my eyes took in everything. Reporters bent over their typewriters, many typing in the old hunt-and-peck style but typing as fast with two fingers as most people could with ten. The rat-a-tat clicking of dozens of typewriters, the distressed aaargh followed by a sharp click as carriages slammed back to the beginning, the rrrrrpppp as paper was snatched from typewriters, the brow-wrinkling quick read of the copy followed by a loud "Copy," all against the backdrop of the brrrrrr of a dozen teletype machines, were a magic elixir that soaked into my being.

I would have to travel to the moon to be any further away from rural southwest Georgia, where I was born. Southwest Georgia is a big bag of rocks on the backs of its children. I had seen it a hundred times: I tell someone where I was born, and a film comes over their eyes, and a tight smile pulls at their mouth. They think I am a dumb Southerner, a cracker, a redneck who knows little about the outside world and whose ideas are from another century. I am defensive and prickly about this. But when I am alone, I wonder if there is some truth to this.

As I waited for the city editor, my thoughts tumbled back down the past six years. Jesus, Joseph, Mary, and the donkey. How could I have made so many terrible decisions? How could I have made so many horrible mistakes? Young men my age have a few victories they can stand upon and dream of their future. They were good students or good athletes in high school or college. They had jobs that either satisfied them or were good platforms from which to jump to bigger jobs.

I had only secrets.

I rubbed my sweaty hands on the legs of my pants, rocked back and forth, and stared straight ahead as my thoughts ricocheted down the past few years.

My story began when I left home to attend North Georgia College in Dahlonega, a mountain hamlet a hundred miles north of Atlanta.

IMAGINE nine acres of whale shit on the bottom of the deepest part of the ocean. Under the whale shit is a layer of primordial goop. And under the primordial goop is where you find freshmen at North Georgia College in the fall of 1955.

We were shapeless, amorphous, civilian blobs, beginning the long and painful process of evolving into officers and gentlemen. Everything that walked, crawled, crept, or flew was superior to us, none more so than sophomores wallowing in their first taste of power.

Think of having to say, "Yes, sir," to a pinch-faced, bug-eyed, drooling sophomore who believed he was a reincarnation of General George Patton. Think of having to stand at rigid attention every time Patton speaks to you; his lips slobber-shiny, elbows bowed out like a berserk rooster, tendons in his neck stretched so tight they're about to pop through his skin. Think of him nose to nose with you, screaming about your ill-fitting uniform, your lack of military presence, the wisp of fuzz on your chin, and how you are the sorriest piece of humanity ever to enroll at the glorious institution that is North Georgia College. And all the while, you know that at any nonmilitary college in America this guy would be getting his ass whipped on a regular basis.

That's the way it was.

Patton intimidated a lot of freshmen. But he didn't bother me. He was a frail and laughable figure measured against my daddy. I had lived under the goop from as far back as I could remember. But now I was at a school that he had always wanted me to attend. Many times, he had told me that if I went to a military school, I would be straightened out. I didn't know what that meant. I was here to find out. I was here to make peace with my dead father.

When I walked in the door at North Georgia, I put aside the dream of becoming a newspaper reporter and maybe even a novelist. It was easy to park the dream because it was so unrealistic. No one from my hometown had ever become a writer. No one from my hometown had ever done much of anything.

From the first day, I knew that me in a military school was like an elevator in an outhouse: I did not belong. I had endured military discipline all of my young life, and I wanted no more. Maybe Patton sensed that. I am certain he sensed that his arm-waving and spit-splattering style did not intimidate me, that I could ride out whatever he could dish out.

To show my disdain for Patton and for school discipline, I went to class once or twice a week. I spent most of my days in a downtown pool hall, and while I became a pretty good pool player, my grades for the first quarter indicated I should never have been admitted. I had a D or an F in every course. When I went home for Thanksgiving, I knew the next quarter would be like the first and that I would flunk out.

While I was at home, Sydney, the girl I had begun dating in high school, told me to take a hike. When she left, so did my judgment.

The next day, I kissed Mother goodbye and stepped out to the road to hitchhike back to Dahlonega. I stopped in Atlanta, called the college, and said I was dropping out. Please pack my goods and ship them to my home address.

I was entering the pinball phase of my life: the years when I bounced around in an erratic and unpredictable fashion, always hoping to find the right slot, but always out of control, bumping, thrown about, then sliding into a trough and rolling down the sluice toward defeat. *Clunk.*

I joined the air force. I have never been able to figure out the line of logic that caused me to drop out of a military college and join the military. Maybe I left the amateurs and joined the professionals. I don't know. But in the South, the military is home: it is where a young man goes when there is no other place to go. We say it is patriotism that motivates us. But it is not. When the world has kicked your ass, when the big unknown is out there waiting to swallow you, when you are terrified of the future, you join the military.

I went to basic training at Lackland Air Force Base in San Antonio, Texas. I had never been so far from home. The people I met were from all across America. Many had what I considered strange ways, and they spoke in accents I had never heard.

We recruits were issued uniforms. When we stepped up to the supply sergeant to receive our shoes, I told him I wore a size five and a half. He looked at my feet, said, "Nope, you wear a seven and a half," and handed me boots and dress shoes.

I looked at my feet and for the first time noticed that the big toe on each foot was curved inward—I mean, a good and obvious curve. For several years, I had been wearing shoes two sizes too small. Even so, when I looked down at my feet shod in my new shoes—shoes that did not squeeze my toes—I was troubled. I was wearing a pair of shoes two sizes bigger than Daddy wore, and in my mind, I was not allowed to have bigger feet than the sarge.

Two weeks into basic training, my company commander called me to his office and chewed my ass out for causing my mother so much worry. She had called North Georgia College, where someone told her I had withdrawn. Somehow Mother had tracked me down. It is the way of mothers to find their offspring, no matter how far they roam.

The company commander ordered me to write Mother and let her know every detail of my life since I had withdrawn from college and when I might be home on leave.

I was hoping the military would teach me discipline and train me to be the master of myself and put me on the road to becoming an exemplary and productive citizen. I had flunked out of college, but I would find redemption in the air force.

Someone once said that wisdom comes from the things we wish had never happened. If that is true, my air force experience would make me the wisest son of a bitch who ever walked.

2

My first posting after basic training was at Fort Belvoir, Virginia, a few miles outside Washington, DC. During the six months I was there, my time was divided into three parts: learning my job, learning to drink, and learning to write.

I did not become proficient in any of the three.

Several dozen young enlisted men from the air force, navy, and army formed my class. We trained to be draftsmen. In what we suspected was motivational blather, the instructors said we were chosen to attend the engineering school because our aptitude tests showed we were among the smartest enlisted troops in the military. But we knew the smartest airmen were selected for the intelligence field.

We learned to draw plans for roads, runways, buildings, schematics, and whatever else the instructors could think of. We even had a class on lettering.

I thought it was still more blather when the instructors said that if we flunked out, we would be assigned to jobs that required only a pulse. The army students would be sent to the infantry. We air force guys would go into POL—petroleum, oil, and lubrication. We would be putting gas into cars, trucks, and airplanes. To use the official job description, we would be "oil checkers." I don't know where the navy men would be sent; I'm guessing guarding brothels in Manila.

On weekends, I learned to drink. The first bar I ever entered was on Fourteenth Street in Washington. I had never had even a beer until I went to Fort Belvoir. The most daring thing I did in Edison was going to a pool hall owned by a man called "Frog." My new friends, several of whom were quite good at this drinking business, advised me that the Singapore Sling was the drink to order. So I ate pizza and guzzled smooth, sweet Singapore Slings until I was nauseated, went outside and around the corner into an alley, and threw up. For a young man in the military, the main thing to know about drinking is knowing where to vomit. After I threw up, a friend said I should order more pizza. "It will line your stomach, and you can drink a lot more," he said.

One Saturday morning, a fellow from an advanced drafting class was part of our group. He was twenty-one, three or four years older than the rest of us. He would point his finger at one of us and lecture as if he knew everything. This guy annoyed the hell out of me. After a while, I got up and wandered down Fourteenth Street, staring into store windows. When I came to a jewelry store, I paused, staring at dozens of rings and watches and necklaces and pendants on little felt display pads. Inside, behind a long glass counter, was a skinny and scowling proprietor whose narrow eyes raked me up and down over my cheap shirt, jeans, white socks, and air force dress shoes. The curl to his lip indicated he knew all there was to know about me.

My southwest Georgia defensiveness blew up out of control. I pushed the door open, walked inside, and ambled from display case to display case, not intending to buy anything, just taking the proprietor's time. Always he moved with me, sidestepping along the glass display case, wearing a tight smile.

I saw a small pendant, a gold heart that was split asunder. I leaned closer to read the engraving on the heart: *mizpah*.

I pointed. "What does that mean? That word on the broken heart."

He unlocked the case and pulled out the small box containing the pendant. He placed it on the countertop and said, "This is not a broken heart. It is one heart in two pieces. *Mizpah* is a biblical word that means, 'The Lord watch between me and thee when we are absent one from another.'"

"What language is *mizpah*?"

He shrugged. "Bible language."

"How much is it?"

He picked up the box and looked at the tag on the bottom. "Ninety dollars." He smiled, knowing I could not afford the piece.

But it must have been a slow Saturday. His face softened a bit, and he said, "Are you military?" My eyes widened, and I asked him how he knew. He said, "I do a lot of business with the military. You fellows have a look about you. Maybe it is your posture."

He nodded and pointed to the pendant. "Give your girlfriend half of the heart, and you wear the other half. When you're not together, you'll be thinking about each other."

I shrugged and mumbled that I had no girl. I almost added that I had been dumped a few months ago, but I decided not to confide that to him.

"You will find a girl soon," he said. He paused and asked if I would like him to put the piece of jewelry on "layaway."

I knew about layaway. People in Edison did that all the time down at Z Israel & Son department store.

I asked him how much down payment he needed; he asked me how much I could afford.

I pulled out my wallet, looked inside, did some quick calculations, and said, "Ten dollars."

"Give it to me. I'll give you a receipt. Can you mail me ten dollars every payday?"

I nodded. He handed me his card that contained his name and the name and address of the store.

Walking back down Fourteenth Street toward the bar, I wondered what the hell was wrong with me. Why did I buy a broken heart? I had no girlfriend. When I finished tech school, I would be shipped overseas. I wasn't sure I could afford taking ten dollars every two weeks from my salary. And yet I was buying jewelry meant for two people.

My first conscious and deliberate effort as a writer began one Saturday morning. I jammed a notebook into the back of my jeans and patted my shirt pocket to make sure two ballpoint pens were there. I stepped out of my barracks and looked around. I was atop a steep hill that sloped down to the Potomac River. Here the river was broad and full and majestic. In high school, I'd learned this was the river associated with George Washington. I looked around but saw no cherry trees, not that I would have recognized one.

I have always been a reader. There was never any discipline to my reading; I read whatever struck my fancy: newspapers, every magazine I could find, historical fiction, books about clipper ships, biographies. I was grasping for some sort of understanding about how to put words together. A few weeks earlier, I had read a passing reference to Thoreau and Emerson. In the base exchange, I bought a paperback book comparing the two men. I often got them confused and couldn't remember which one wrote what. But the story of Thoreau going into the woods and living at Walden Pond for a year resonated with me. I thought of Thoreau as a hermit, a man who told the world to kiss his ass. I didn't understand Emerson and the transcendentalist business, but I liked his rebellious side.

Since I'd arrived at Fort Belvoir, I had been scribbling in a note-book, short scenes, a bit of dialogue, or puny efforts at poetry. The value of these scribblings was that they kept alive the smoldering coals of desire to one day be a writer. Today I wanted to write, but I did not know what to write about. Since Emerson was on my mind, I decided to write a poem to Emerson.

I had read of the enormous discipline it takes to write poetry. I needed discipline . . . in many areas.

My plan for this morning caused a great internal battle, an old and familiar battle. Had the sarge known about today, he would have snorted in derision and said I was in the military and I should be learning how to kill the enemies of America, not wandering in the woods and engaging in a dandified and frivolous pursuit.

I was running toward the sarge even as I ran away from him. My steps were faltering because he had been a dominating influ-ence in my life and my mother's life and, to a lesser degree, in the lives of my two brothers and my sister. Sergeant J. B. Coram had been forty when he'd married seventeen-year-old Augusta Buie of Fayetteville, North Carolina. This great age difference meant she never achieved equal footing in the marriage. The sarge was a romping, stomping, overbearing, even frightening disciplinarian. When he died at fifty-nine, Mother was a very young thirty-six. I was sixteen, and I felt not the slightest remorse about not mourning for Daddy. His death was the most liberating event in my young life. And now, on this cool, clear day in northern Virginia, I was seeking a new world.

I moved among the trees and brush, always angling down the ridge. After ten minutes, I found a spot from where I could see a long and open expanse of river. The Potomac was blue and sparkled in the morning sun, sending pulses of light through the air. The woods smelled old, but at the same time, there was a crispness in the air that hinted of the coming spring. I heard songbirds.

I stood there a long moment looking down the river. I sighed and pulled the notebook from under my jacket, sat on a bare spot of dirt, crossed my legs, and tapped a pen on the notebook. I was Emerson, alone in the woods. I wrinkled my brow. I scrunched up my mouth. I stared at the sky. I wrote and scratched out. I wrote and scratched out. And over the next two hours, I came up with my "Ode to Emerson."

> *Here am I, Emerson,*
> *On the banks of this famous stream*
> *Where other men of destiny*
> *Have come to sit and dream.*
>
> *I too will not conform*
> *To society's unreal world.*
> *But will live my life as I please,*
> *'til the flag of death unfurls.*
>
> *And if you happen to look down*
> *From your high and kingly seat,*
> *Know that I am following thee*
> *Until man on earth with God doth meet.*

I offer this because it was my first poem and the first thing I ever wrote that was not a class assignment.

As 1 looked down at the poem, I felt the sarge looking at me and laughing in ridicule. I climbed the hill and walked through the woods to my barracks.

3

THE overweight sergeant looked at my friend and me in the dismissive, almost contemptuous, manner that old sergeants have when dealing with junior enlisted men. He was bored, burned out, and counting the days until retirement. He sighed, pulled a coin from his pocket, held it up for us to see, and said, "Okay, one of you yard birds call it. Winner gets his choice."

I looked at my friend. We had graduated from engineering school, had a month of leave, flown across the Atlantic, and now we were in an air force processing center near London. Two air force bases in England needed draftsmen, and the sergeant was trying to decide who to send to what base. One assignment was at an air force base on the east side of England facing the North Sea. The second was at Brize Norton, a Strategic Air Command (SAC) base near Oxford. The sergeant said that whoever went to Brize Norton would be on a SAC base but not in SAC, rather in a tenant squadron about which he knew nothing. He called it the Thirtieth Supply Squadron Depot Specialists, but he didn't know what the squadron supplied or what they put in a depot. It all sounded so ordinary, but it wasn't, because whoever went to Brize Norton would need a top security clearance. Spooky shit going on down there.

My friend shook his head in disbelief. This sergeant was going to decide our first assignment, and by extension, influence the remaining years of our enlistment with a coin toss?

I nodded for him to make the call. "Heads," he said.

The slab-faced sergeant flipped the coin, snatched it out of the air with speed born of long experience, turned it over on the back of his large, freckled hand, lifted his hand, and said, "Tails." He turned to me. "Where do you want to go?"

"Brize Norton."

And it was by that rigid and technical selection process that I was assigned to the Thirtieth SSDS at Brize Norton. The squadron was located on the edge of a taxiway in a remote corner of the base and was behind a double row of high fences topped with barbed wire. Spaced at regular intervals along the fence were towers manned by vigilant and stern-faced air policemen armed with automatic weapons and side arms.

Until I received my clearance, I could not work inside the compound. The military does not like for the troops to sit around doing nothing. Idle hands and all that. To fill my time, I was sent to school to learn how to drive military vehicles. The license enabled me to drive on the base. When I graduated, I was sent to another school to learn how to drive on the roads of England. When I finished that school, I was awarded an off-base driving license.

I did not realize it at the time, but having a license to drive a military vehicle was a big deal. Having an off-base license was even bigger. I was an airman third class, and in England, very few junior enlisted people, except those who worked in the motor pool, had such a license. The irony was that I went to driving school because there was nothing else for me to do.

Back home, a young FBI agent conducting my background check had roamed around Edison for a week, asking if I had Communist leanings. People in Edison didn't know what a Communist was, but they knew it was not a good thing. They told the FBI agent about my dad having been a career army sergeant, said they had known me all my life, and as far as they knew, I was not a Communist. Given that I had just turned eighteen, there was not much of my life that could be suspect. The FBI agent signed off on me, the paperwork made its way through the air force, and I had a top secret security clearance.

Now I could be admitted to the inner sanctum. The squadron's first sergeant—the senior enlisted man in the squadron—gave me the tour. He was tall, slim, unsmiling, and had great command presence. He wore more stripes than a zebra, chevrons on his upper arm and hash marks on the lower. And he had a chest full of medals. Another Daddy Rabbit.

His eyes had the impassive hardness that comes from years in the military. I wondered if he had children and if they had lived difficult lives. I knew from my own experience that children spawned by a career military man often have painful childhoods. The scars are deep and can be lasting.

Many military men do not know how to show love and affection. Or if they do, they do it in such a manner that it is not recognized. The sarge looked on me not as his son, but as a raw recruit who needed iron discipline and a deep understanding of the things that were important: patriotism, sense of duty, never making excuses, doing the job no matter the obstacles, and the awareness there were causes worth dying for. This was his code. And when I rejected the code, when I rejected all that the sarge stood for, I rejected the most priceless gift a father can give to his son.

Now I was standing in front of another sergeant with the same code. Among the first sergeant's many responsibilities was the job of getting every new airman squared away and impressing him with the need for good behavior.

As a symbol of authority, generals and first sergeants were authorized to carry a swagger stick, a polished stick about eighteen inches long. The ends were topped with silver or ivory. Carrying the swagger stick was optional, and most generals and almost all sergeants elected not to do so. My first sergeant carried a swagger stick.

The first sergeant met me at the gate, signed me in, and we walked toward the side door of an enormous hangar. He said that after I was photographed, I would have a badge that I would wear at all times when I was in the compound.

With his eyes straight ahead, he said, "And you will get rid of that duck-ass haircut. You will present a sharp military appearance in this squadron."

I had let my hair grow during my month-long leave before coming to England. Now it was long and swept back and had the appearance of . . . well, a ducktail.

"Yes, First Sergeant."

We walked into a cavernous office space with about a dozen desks. Two desks were staffed by officers, the remainder by enlisted men. On the left was a glassed office, and a sign on the door said, "Squadron Commander."

This was my first job in the air force, and I had the normal apprehension plus the curiosity in being assigned to the Thirtieth. What did they do here that required a security clearance? Could I do what the air force required of me? Was I as good as the other men in the big office?

As can most first sergeants, this first sergeant had the ability to read the mind of an enlisted man. "You will meet all these people in due course," he said. "Right now you need to know what we do here." He pushed open a door on the side of the large room, and we walked into a cavernous hangar.

Throughout the hangar, dozens of gray-painted bombs rested on wheeled carts. Some of the bombs were small—two or three feet long—and rested on a cart at eye level. Some bombs had open side panels revealing the innards. The bombs were of different lengths and sizes, but all looked like regular bombs: cylindrical objects tapering toward rear fins. Enlisted men with screwdrivers and wrenches and other small tools were bent over the bombs. More bombs were lined up in rows against the back wall of the hangar.

The first sergeant swept his swagger stick across the full view and in a very proud voice asked if I had ever seen an atomic bomb.

I almost said, "Yeah, I played with them all the time when I was growing up in southwest Georgia." But I sensed the first sergeant's sense of humor was not well developed, so I said what he expected me to say. "No, First Sergeant."

He said I was looking at more than three dozen atomic weapons, both tactical and strategic, and that the Thirtieth was a depot for the storage and maintenance of atomic weapons throughout Europe.

He looked at me and waited for my reaction. What the hell did he expect me to say? I was looking at enough atomic bombs to turn Europe into a sheet of glass. All that came to mind was "Is every one of these an atomic bomb?"

The sergeant said these were garden-variety atomic bombs, but on occasion, a plutonium bomb arrived for maintenance. He chuckled to show me that sergeants know about everything, including nuclear fission. He said when a plutonium bomb exploded, they "blast out some bad stuff." Sort of like severe radiation. But worse.

I had nothing to say.

The Thirtieth was one of only three such squadrons in the air force, the first sergeant said. There was one in North Africa and one in the States. He turned and looked at me. "You are about to be promoted to airman second class. The men who have your job in the other squadrons are sergeants."

I think he was telling me I was lucky to be here.

He leaned toward me and in an intense voice said my job as the squadron draftsman would be to design and draw new parts, replacement parts, or modifications for nuclear weapons that came to the squadron. He said I would also be called upon to draw schematics for the complex circuitry of the bombs.

Schematics. I had a visceral loathing for schematics. These byzantine yet precise electrical drawings almost caused me to flunk out of tech school. I understood nothing about electricity except that when you flip up a switch, the lights turn on. Flip it down, and the lights turn off.

The sergeant handed me a small black plastic box with a short, lightweight chain attached.

"Dosimeter," he said. "Measures the amount of radioactivity in your immediate vicinity. Thread the chain through a buttonhole. You will wear it at all times when inside the security fence." He paused and pointed his swagger stick toward me. "Young airman, if that thing ever starts clicking, you get the hell away from wherever you are. The faster it clicks, the faster you run. Chances are you will never hear it click. But if it does, you report directly to me or to an officer."

I held the dosimeter up and looked at it. "What would make it click?" I asked.

"A radiation leak. But don't worry. It has never happened here."

The first sergeant was still pointing his swagger stick at me and said that during his career, he had held a number of jobs, one of which was a draftsman. He said that if I thought that just because I was the single draftsman in the squadron, I could coast a bit in my work, I should rethink my situation. He knew good work when he saw it, and if he had to, he could do my job. He would be looking over my shoulder.

When I was growing up, the sarge would issue orders, and the acceptable response was "Yes, sir." Well, there was also "No, sir" and "No, excuse, sir." Sergeants are not built to communicate. They are built to impose order. So when the first sergeant finished his speech and looked at me, I said, "Yes, First Sergeant."

I was looking at several dozen atomic bombs. I had no frame of reference for this and was torn between thinking it was all some sort of cosmic joke or wondering what the hell I was doing in this place. The military places awful responsibilities on young and inexperienced men.

"One more thing," the first sergeant said.

I looked up at him.

In a voice half sarcastic and half contemptuous, he said I was too young to appreciate what he was about to tell me, but that I should know the nearby town of Oxford was one of the most famous towns in the world. "You can go into Oxford every day after work if you want to," he said. On the weekend, London is less than two hours away. The west end of London is a young man's dream. It is filled with whores, pimps, and snake charmers.

He was trying to tell me that not only did I have one of the most prestigious jobs a young airman can have, but also my choices of where to go when I was off duty were as good those available to any airman anywhere in the world.

I was still numb from thinking about atomic bombs. The first sergeant poked me with his swagger stick and in a disgusted voice said, "You have no idea what the hell I am saying to you."

"Yes, First Sergeant. I understand."

"One other thing you better understand."

I waited.

He waved his swagger stick. "Do you know what this is?"

"A swagger stick, First Sergeant."

"Noooooo," he said, his voice leaking sarcasm. "It is a magic wand."

I waited.

He said if he pointed the stick at me and said my living area should be ready for inspection at all times, then, by God, my living area would be ready for inspection at all times.

"Yes, First Sergeant."

His face pruned up, and he looked angry when he said that at all times I would demonstrate the superior performance and exemplary behavior expected from a member of this elite squadron. He said I would produce professional work and do it fast.

He raised his eyebrows and waited for the acceptable response.

"Yes, First Sergeant." I could do this all day and never break a sweat.

He pursed his lips and rocked on his heels. "One more thing. People on base will ask you what you do here. People are curious about the Thirtieth. They know we are not part of SAC, and we sure as hell are not a regular air force squadron. We work behind security fences and armed air policemen. Anybody who asks, tell them you work in a supply squadron. And that is all you tell them."

"Yes, First Sergeant."

He said that even in my Quonset hut, which I shared with more than a dozen other men from the squadron, I would not talk about my job.

"Yes, First Sergeant."

"Make damned sure. Because air force investigators are planted throughout this squadron." He grimaced as if he smelled something unpleasant. "I don't know who they are. Those sneaky bastards have regular jobs, but their real job is to keep an eye on us. You will be a target for those guys because you are the only draftsman in the squadron. You even hint at what you draw on your drawing board or that nuclear weapons are stored in our hangar, and for the rest of your life, you will be at Leavenworth making little rocks out of big rocks."

He raised his eyebrows.

"Yes, First Sergeant."

So, there I was, an eighteen-year-old kid who had flunked out of college, a green and naive kid with an underdeveloped sense of responsibility; a redneck Southerner with a nonexistent worldview, and I had a top secret security clearance and a job drawing modifications for atomic bombs. Every aspect of my work was classified.

And I could go to London on weekends.

God bless America.

4

Atomic bombs were not my big revelation in England. Women were my big revelation.

In England, chastity disappeared sometime around the Middle Ages. I found that sex was the way British girls said hello. I'm not complaining. I say long live the British Empire and hooray for the blokes. All Brits, no matter their gender, we called blokes. And the bloke girls made it simple for me. Back home, there were good girls and bad girls. We married the good girls. The bad girls, we parked with in the woods. There was a clear line of distinction between good girls and bad girls. In England, that line disappeared.

English women introduced me to casual sex. Often, weekends found a friend and me along with two girls we had picked up in a pub, banging away in the same hotel room, sometimes in the same bed. In fair weather, I had sex out in open fields. I had hand jobs in movie theaters. I was introduced to wall jobs on a side street in London. And it was under a pub table in the ancient and venerated city of Oxford that I had my first blow job. Oxford is indeed a city of learning.

English girls believed they could fuck their way to the good old USA. And many did. All too often, an eighteen- or nineteen-year-old boy, away from home for the first time, got homesick, got laid, mistook sex for love, and married a bloke. All his friends made note of his hometown back in the States and said they would look him up after they got out of the air force.

An enlisted airman who wanted to marry a bloke needed permission from his squadron commander. Eighteen-year-old boys seized in grand passion knew permission would be denied, so they did not ask. Punishment for marrying without permission was being confined to the base for a month. And every day the young enlisted man was confined, he fretted that his bloke wife might be getting to know another American.

Because my squadron dealt with nuclear weapons, we had a high percentage of enlisted men with college degrees. Several had engineering degrees. Those of us who had not graduated looked up to them. They were smooth, pulled literary and historical references into their conversation, and they were at ease talking with officers. They talked of things I did not know about. And I did not know that I did not know of those things until I heard them brought into a conversation. But one thing I did know: a college education made a difference in a person. It added not just knowledge but depth, self-confidence, and polish—attributes I did not have. It was from the college graduates that I learned I was mispronouncing many words. Because I read so much as a young boy, I knew words that I had never heard pronounced. I learned that *Bermuda* was not pronounced "Bermooda." I learned that *Bedouin* was not pronounced "be-DOW-in." And I learned that *Hawaii* was not pronounced "Hi-WHY-yuh."

The college graduates were amused by my mispronunciations. And from their casual remarks, I gathered that Southerners were considered slow, dumb, and clueless, anthropological specimens from "down there." In large part, this was due to our accents. The conversation of a boy from the Bronx might be mutilated beyond recognition, but his speech was not connected to his intelligence. A Mexican kid from Texas might speak in such accented English that only a word here and there could be understood. But everyone assumed he was a normal guy and his mastery of English would come with time. The gnarly speech of a boy from Maine never raised an eyebrow. But a Southern accent brought universal scorn.

It brought some amusement to those in my Quonset hut that I read so much. But the college boys encouraged me. In England, my love for books exploded. Maybe it was because of radiation leaking from the atomic bombs. I don't know. I read without discipline: novels and nonfiction, the classics I would have read in college, everything. Even the freewheeling British newspapers.

It was as a young enlisted man in England that I discovered Tom Paine, the writer who kept the American Revolution alive with his incendiary pamphlets. He was an improbable man to achieve such prominence. He was from England and worked as a corset maker before going to the colonies. He was a common man, rough-hewn, and his prose was hammered out on the anvil of freedom. His gut-bucket writing was read by firelight in the camps of Valley Forge, and Washington's soldiers found it powerful beyond words. I read *Common Sense* many times and saw how simple words formed into simple sentences could have unimaginable power. When I read *The American Crisis*, I wondered if I would ever again read such transcendent opening lines as, "These are the times that try men's souls. The summer soldier and the sunshine patriot will, in this crisis, shrink from the service of their country; but he that stands by it now, deserves the love and thanks of man and woman." I have not.

One of the college men in my Quonset hut pointed out that we were a few miles from Oxford, where C. S. Lewis and J. R. R. Tolkien—men I had never heard of—had worked. Those men belonged to a group of writers called the Inklings, which I thought a clever name. I read several Lewis books, which pointed me back to the Bible. The King James version was the basis for every sermon preached in the Edison Baptist Church. As is the way of young men, I began to question my childhood religion.

I resolved to finish college when my enlistment ended. In the meantime, one way that I compensated—as did several of my fellow illiterates—was by wearing custom-made clothes. This is what the college graduates did, and we followed their example. A number of English tailors set up business on the base or just outside the gates. These were not Saville Row tailors but hucksters preying on naive young airmen. Their materials were inferior, and their work was of poor quality. But I did not know that. I knew that they sewed my name inside a coat and my initials on a shirt. And I thought that was the most stylish thing I had ever encountered.

For many of us, especially if we were from the South, the first piece of custom clothing we bought was a topcoat. We had never had a need for a topcoat. But English winters were cold. In fact, most of the time, it was cold in England. A custom-made topcoat was our chance to be smooth and urbane.

Mine was navy blue with tiny flecks of gray. It was a heavy horse blanket of a coat. It must have weighed ten pounds. But it was warm.

One Saturday morning, a half dozen of us were at the train station waiting for the train to London. We Americans clustered in a group, passing around a bottle of whiskey, taking surreptitious drinks, then hiding the bottle under a topcoat. The blokes on the platform were filled with inherent superiority and often cut their eyes toward us, their gaze lingering and accompanied by the standard superior smile. Some grimaced at our loudness, our drinking, our profanity, and our comments on all things British. We did not care. But I did wonder what the hell was the matter with them. Blokes have manners. They do not stare at strangers.

The train arrived, and there was the usual scrum as we tried to figure out which compartment we could take over. We Americans wanted our own compartment. I was the last one aboard and swung into a seat near the door.

When we arrived in London, I was the first one out the door. And as I exited, I heard loud laughter from my friends. "Take off your coat and look at the back of it," one said.

A streak of pigeon shit began at the edge of my collar and cascaded down my back in a great white spear. It had been there long enough, pressed in by the seat back, that it would never come out.

While we had been at the station waiting on the train to London, a pigeon on one of the overhead crossbeams had been saving his shit for an American. He saw me and aimed for my head. It was a near miss.

My office had glass walls on three sides. The squadron commander and I were the only people with glass-enclosed offices.

On shelves along the rear of my office were manuals for every nuclear weapon in the air force inventory: tactical and strategic bombs and artillery shells. Every manual was classified as top secret. Except for the list of nuclear targets inside the Soviet Union, there was not much in the air force with a higher classification than these manuals.

These books were my bibles. They guided my work. I was not a good draftsman. I could do the basic stuff, but little about my job was basic. It was technical and precise and detailed. My job had more than a little cachet, but it did not interest me. I was not then and am not now excited about drawing a cross section of a runway or trying to understand a schematic. God, I hated schematics.

But I liked having the manuals in my office. Because these manuals often were open atop my drafting table, no one could enter my office unless they had the need to know what I was working on. That was the squadron commander, the first sergeant, and an electrical engineer from the hangar.

Anytime I stepped outside my office, I locked the door. If I walked to the latrine, I locked the door. If I went to the chow hall, I locked the door.

I was King Shit, and I knew it.

But in the back of my mind was a refrain I'd heard often when I was growing up, something the sarge liked to remind me of: "You will never amount to anything."

Since the sarge was always right, the next step in my air force career was to fuck up.

5

One Friday afternoon I was returning from the chow hall, and as I unlocked my office, I heard a tapping on the glass across the hall. I looked over my shoulder and saw the squadron commander beckoning me.

The captain was a quiet and studious man, slender, with dark hair, and he wore round steel-framed military-issued glasses. He was a mild and low-key fellow with a soft voice. Among the enlisted ranks, there was talk he had been passed over for promotion. If he were passed over again, he would be forced to retire.

In front of his desk, I came to attention.

"At ease," he said with a wave. He took off his glasses, looked at me for a moment, and said, "Airman Coram, I have a job for you. Put aside whatever else you are doing because this has top priority. Go to the first sergeant, and he will give you the details. But know that what he says comes from me and that this will be the most important job of your career."

"Yes, sir."

"Do your best, airman." From his tone and his demeanor, the captain was invested in this job—whatever it was.

The first sergeant saw me come out of the captain's office. He pointed toward my office, followed me inside, closed the door, and from under his arm, withdrew a loose-leaf notebook. He opened to a marked page and out flopped a multifold schematic. The schematic draped across my desk and fell to the floor. The sergeant tapped the schematic with a long bony finger, stared at me, and said, "This is it."

"Yes, First Sergeant." I had no idea what he was talking about.

I picked up a few pages and saw the most complicated schematic I had ever seen: a tangled mass of circuitry for a new model of atomic bomb, one designed to penetrate reinforced concrete before exploding. It was designed for use against Soviet submarine pens and was the first of what, decades later and in a far more sophisticated iteration, would be known as a "bunker buster."

"Airman, your job is to enlarge this schematic," the first sergeant said. "Make it big enough to tack up on the wall so those wizards out there"—he jerked his thumb over his shoulder toward the hangar—"can read it from ten feet away."

I looked at the schematic and shook my head. This one had to be perfect. If the electrical wiring for an atomic bomb is not faultless . . . well, you can figure that one out.

"Airman, listen carefully. General LeMay is flying in tomorrow, and the CO wants this rendering for the new bomb available to the general."

General Curtis LeMay commanded the Strategic Air Command. He was a cigar-smoking, impatient man. He had fired more colonels than any other general in the air force. His quick and forceful decisions made him universally feared. If America went to war, it would be General LeMay's bombers that led the attack. Now he was checking to make sure that his nuclear weapons in England were updated and ready to launch.

The first sergeant continued. "Your rendering must be clean and crisp and sharp. No wavy lines. No inkblots. It must be perfect. Do you understand what I am saying to you?"

"Yes, First Sergeant."

I eyed the schematic and computed how long the job would take. "Twelve hours," said the first sergeant, reading my mind. "Maybe fourteen. That means you have to get started now. You should finish before daylight."

I scratched my cheek, sighed, and said, "First Sergeant, it is Friday night, and I . . ." My voice trailed off.

He looked at me in disgust. "A woman."

I nodded.

I had fallen in love with a little redhead named Sarah. We had met several weeks earlier at one of the big Saturday dances held in every community. Since then, we had seen each other every night. She lived in council housing about a mile outside the front gate of the base. She was the first girl I had felt affection for since Sydney had dumped me. I told myself she was different from other English girls. She was seventeen, and she moaned when we kissed, and she pulled me close, but she would not go to a hotel with me. "I've never done that before," she said. "I'm afraid."

I had found the last remaining virgin in Great Britain.

Sarah wore tight white sweaters, and her hair gleamed as if caught in a searchlight. Plus, she shaved her armpits, something British girls seldom did. My friends envied me and said she was the best-looking bloke they had ever seen. And I believed that tonight would be the night.

I had made regular payments to the jeweler on Fourteenth Street in Washington, and now I owed him only ten dollars. I wanted the gold heart inscribed with *mizpah*, and I wanted to give half of it to Sarah. I sent a wire to the jeweler asking if he would mail me the necklace, that I would send him the remaining ten dollars next month. He said no. I wired back for him to return my money. He said no.

About fifteen minutes from the front gate at Brize Norton was a little pub on the banks of the Thames. Great, white, elegant swans glided up and down the river. Above the pub, three rooms were available for rent. I reserved a corner room overlooking the river and had dreams of waking up Saturday morning in that room with Sarah in my arms.

"Sarge," I groaned.

His lips squeezed together as tight as if he were a Baptist preacher. He thumped me on the arm with his swagger stick and said, "Airman, you remember what this is?"

"A swagger stick, First Sergeant."

"No, dammit. I already told you. It is a magic wand."

I nodded.

"Airman, if I tell you to stay at your desk until you finish this goddamn rendering, you will stay at your desk until you finish the goddamn rendering."

"Yes, First Sergeant."

The first sergeant caressed the sleek surface of his swagger stick and with a satisfied grin on his lined face, said, "See? It is magic."

He turned and walked to the door. Over his shoulder, he said, "Lots of bloke women out there, young airman. You stay here until you finish that rendering. The captain's ass is on the line. My ass is on the line. Your ass is on the line. I'm going to have the company clerk bring you something from the chow hall tonight. Except for going to the latrine—and don't do that too often—you will not leave your desk until you finish the job. Do you read me?"

"Yes, First Sergeant."

He closed the door and kept his burning glare turned on me. I thought his glare might melt the glass. But then he turned and walked down the hall, snapping his swagger stick against his open hand.

I looked at my watch. Thirteen thirty in military parlance. One thirty to me. With a twelve-hour job in front of me, there was no way I could make my date with Sarah.

Maybe she had plans to get married and go to the States with me. I don't know. But if she wanted me to say I loved her before we went to bed, I would do that. I would say I was a secret agent and in training to go to the moon and that General LeMay was a homosexual. Whatever it took.

At 4:00 p.m., the office emptied. Many of my squadron mates would soon race for the train and ride to the west end of London. Other squadron mates would walk out the main gate to one of the half-dozen nearby pubs. It was at one of those pubs where Sarah and I were to have drinks, dinner, more drinks, and then, if the planets were aligned and cosmic forces were bending in my favor, we would get in a cab and drive a few minutes, talking of mundane things, until we checked into the pub on the banks of the Thames.

I bent over the schematic. It was slow and tedious work, and the drafting pen had a tendency to squirt blobs of ink if it were not loaded just so. General LeMay did not like blobs.

Around seven thirty, the squadron phone began ringing. No one else was in the hangar, so I ignored it. But it rang and rang and rang. I walked across the hangar, picked up the phone, and said, "Thirtieth SSDS. Airman Coram, sir."

"Don't 'sir' me, asshole," said a voice I recognized. Sammy was from South Carolina, and his bunk was above mine. Often, we talked until late into the night.

"What do you want?"

"She is here, and she is asking about you. Man, she looks good. She is wearing that white sweater, and her titties look so hard she must have dipped them in ice water."

"Come on, Sammy. She's my girlfriend."

"Well, your girlfriend is not wearing a brassiere tonight. She wants to know where you are. Says you two had a date. What do you want me to tell her?"

"Tell her I'm working all night and didn't know how to get in touch with her. I don't even know if she has a phone. Tell her I will see her tomorrow night; same place, same time." I bent my head. "Damn, I hate this."

"Hey, I'm going to tell her I couldn't find you, that you forgot your date. If she wants to cry on my shoulder, I will let her."

"Sammy, don't do that."

Click.

I slammed the phone down again and again.

After that, my work went to hell. Straight lines got the wobbles. Lettering lost its consistency. Numbers lost the baseline. And . . . I had blobs.

About 10:00 p.m., I put my pen down, locked my office, and walked out. I would tell the first sergeant I got sick. Which was true. I was sick with the thought that Sammy had snaked my little redhead. This had happened to me three times in high school. Other boys had taken away my girlfriends. Then Sydney had dumped me. The pain of those times remained fresh, and tonight had ripped the top off still bloody wounds.

At the Quonset hut, I put on jeans, caught a bus to the main gate, nodded to the air policeman, and hurried toward the pub.

One of the squadron maintenance sergeants, an electrical wizard from the hangar, saw me going through the gate and called the first sergeant to ask if I had finished the rendering.

The first sergeant left his family and grumbled his way across the base to my office. There he summed up his rusty skills as a draftsman. His work was as messy as mine. Maybe more so. But sometime before dawn, he finished the schematic. It did not even rise to the level of being mediocre. He knew it. And he knew that General LeMay would know.

Sarah was not in the pub. I became knee-walking drunk and felt the bitter and heartsick feeling of once again being betrayed, of having a girl leave me, of being abandoned.

How I got back to the base, I do not know. All I remember is that I awakened about 10:00 a.m. Saturday with a thundering head, a roiling stomach, and the sure and certain feeling of impending disaster.

I did not pause to shower and shave. I put on my fatigues, caught a bus across base, waved my ID at the security guard, and opened the door.

The first sergeant saw me, marched up to me, and for a minute I thought he was going to lash me with his swagger stick. He was quivering with controlled rage. He leaned down until we were nose to nose and in a tight voice said, "You are relieved of duty, busted to airman basic, and confined to your quarters until further notice."

My first thought was that he was overreacting. Busted to an airman slick sleeve? A little extreme. I had walked out on my job. But he had fixed it. Why the harsh reaction? Before I had time to react, he leaned closer and said, "And your security clearance is suspended."

"Yes, Sergeant Major." I was about to turn away.

In a disgusted and disappointed tone, he added, "Your squadron commander has been relieved of duty. General LeMay fired him. Thanks to you, the captain is out of the air force." Now his lips were quivering with rage. "And a letter of criticism has been placed in my personnel file. I am two years away from retirement, and because of you, I have the first disciplinary act of my twenty-eight-year career."

I could not speak. The ripples from my walking away from my desk were washing up on shores I could not even imagine. I was a little pissant junior enlisted man—now, very junior—and had caused damage I could not begin to understand.

"Get out of my sight."

A few hours later, the squadron clerk accompanied by an air policeman came to my Quonset hut and handed me a set of orders. I was transferred to Burtonwood, up near Manchester, and assigned to a POL squadron. Immediate meant immediate. The air police-man told me to pack, that his orders were to take me to the train station in Oxford and to stay there until I boarded a train and the train left the station.

When I said there was someone off base that I wanted to say goodbye to, the air policeman said, "My orders are to take you to the train station. You will make no stops en route."

I was not allowed to say goodbye to Sarah. In a single day, I had gone from having one of the best jobs an enlisted man could have to a job pumping gas. I was transferred from an air force base near the beautiful and historic town of Oxford to a base in the grimy industrial north of England. I was moved from a squadron of bright and ambitious young men to a squadron of losers and shit birds.

And I had written nothing since the ode to Emerson. I had made no progress toward becoming a writer.

6

My POL career began at RAF Burtonwood, a big rambling air force base located about halfway between Manchester and Liverpool. A few miles from the base, on the banks of the Mersey, was the town of Warrington, where on weeknights the airmen of Burtonwood swaggered into local pubs to complain about warm beer and to deflower whatever virgins might remain in this part of England. On weekends, we invaded the much larger town of Manchester. We stayed away from Liverpool because that was a rough seaport town and a place where a young American could get his ass kicked.

Most of the air traffic at Burtonwood were big four-engine transports either landing with a load of airmen assigned to England or taking off with a load of airmen returning home. Then there was a weather squadron that flew old B-29s.

Big rotary engines pulling big aircraft across the Atlantic require a great deal of fuel. And that is where I came in. The fuel trucks came and went from the POL shack, a small, two-room structure on the back side of the flight line. Even in the summer, which was the third Tuesday of July, the window of the POL shack was closed. Yet the pervasive smell of JP-4 jet fuel and high-octane aviation fuel permeated the air. The smell lingered in my clothes, and when I went to the chow hall, many wrinkled their noses.

The POL shack was a bit different from my former glassed-in office. A desk, a straight-backed wooden chair, and two ratty, overstuffed chairs furnished the front room. In the back room was a two-burner stove used by civilian bloke employees to brew their tea. An open shower with six showerheads was against one wall. In the corner was a toilet. No wall or cubicle surrounded the toilet, which meant we had to do our business in full view of whoever was in the line shack. I hated that. A man should be able to do his business in private. The toilet is a place for contemplation, a place to think profound thoughts.

But the military believes that bodily functions and showering are done in public.

Because I was so junior in rank, and because I was the newbie, I worked the night shift and weekends. The POL shack was my kingdom.

I liked night work because the air traffic lessened and the flight line was quiet. Manning the POL shack was a one-man job. When truck drivers came to have their trucks refilled, I signed a form, made a note of their truck number and how much gas they pumped, and that was that.

My previous job as a draftsman was a job that evoked respect and envy. My new job could have been done by a child. When I told someone I worked in POL, a look came over their face that showed they thought I was one of the dumbest guys in the air force. Working in POL and being a Southerner put me at the bottom of the air force social order.

No chance of ever seeing my friend General LeMay on this job. And I must have been one of the few airman slick sleeves working at POL who once had held a top secret security clearance.

My boss was Sergeant Luther Walling, a lanky, shifty-eyed man from West Virginia who spoke with one of those unmistakable mountain accents. He was in his forties and terrified that something might happen to reduce him in rank or take away his retirement benefits. He was an anxious man, jittery and jerky, always looking over his shoulder while he awaited Armageddon.

I was on the job but a few days when he called in the middle of the night, using what he thought was a disguised voice, and identified himself as "Mr. Tucker." He said he was a civilian passing through Warrington, and he wondered what sort of aircraft the air force had parked on the ramp.

I looked out the window and said that all I could see was a half-dozen or so B-29s and a couple of refueling tankers but that I suspected a number of transports were across the flight line at base operations. "You want me to go out and look around and see if I can identify some more?"

Anything to please Mr. Tucker.

He hung up.

Five minutes later, he called back but this time identified himself as Sergeant Walling and said I had committed a major security breach, that no one outside the air force had any business knowing what aircraft were parked on the ramp. It did no good when I said I had recognized his voice earlier and knew he was posing as Mr. Tucker.

"No way," he said. "You couldn't have recognized my voice."

Twang, twang.

The sergeant made it sound as if he were granting me a special favor when he said he would not turn me in for violating operational security. "If I do this, henceforth, I expect your loyalty on all matters."

"Sarge, you have my loyalty."

"No, I mean your complete loyalty."

"Sarge, I don't understand."

"You will. You will."

He hung up, and I went back to work wondering if he was a complete whack job. But then, if POL was made up of dimwits and screwups, it made sense that the air force would send in supervisors who were advanced dimwits and screwups. The sarge had been in POL his entire career, and his brain was pickled by gas fumes. Yet what remained of my air force career depended on his whims and institutionalized paranoia.

I supervised two civilians who did manual labor and odd jobs around the flight line. One of these men was a tall, disjointed Irishman who—like many Irishmen—talked a lot. And—again like many Irishmen—kept Guinness in his two-quart thermos. The other was a bloke about five feet tall, a half-witted little man with a perpetual smile who walked around saying, "Vice," every few seconds. He drew out the word so it sounded like "Viiiiiiiiice," and he nodded and looked around as if he had just shared the secret of the universe.

Working the night shift in a little shack on the far edge of the flight line was a bleak and enervating existence: menial, repetitious, and boring. The people who drove the fuel trucks were the people I had grown up with in southwest Georgia: defensive, angry, quick to fight, not too bright, and pissed off at the world and everyone in it.

The flight line was cold, and the wind never stopped blowing. Nights were long. But those nights gave me the chance to read. I bought a small satchel that I carried to work every night. It contained candy bars and several books. My reading remained undisciplined and erratic. But occasionally I found a book that did what books are supposed to do: they lingered in my heart. And their words and phrases cascaded across my mind.

One of those books was *Generation of Vipers* by Phillip Wylie. The book had been published more than a decade earlier and gone through numerous reprints. Wylie had the sharpest and most slashing wit I had ever read. He wrote phrases I would remember all my life. In one chapter, he attacked moms and what he called "momism" and said that a dozen or so moms did not have enough sex appeal to budge a hermit ten paces off a rock ledge. He talked of women whose urine would etch glass. He offended just about anyone who could be offended, and because I was young, because I was an empty vessel, I was drawn to his clever vitriol and his smart-assed comments. At night, as the red-and-green wingtip lights of aircraft pulsed through the window and the powerful stab of landing lights turned the office to daylight, I leaned back in my chair, propped my feet on my desk, and read Phillip Wylie aloud. I laughed and rolled his pepper-laden phrases around on my tongue and dreamed of the day when I might write such prose.

One night I read a passing reference to the *Kama Sutra*, an ancient Sanskrit treatise on the art of love. The book is revered in academic circles as the master of its genre. And the drawings, which are always mentioned, are done by masters. I was nineteen, and this was a book I wanted to read. The book was not in the base library. The librarian in Warrington said she did not have the book, but I would find it at the John Rylands Library in Manchester.

I had never heard of the John Rylands Library. But if they had the *Kama Sutra*, then that was where I would go.

One foggy Monday morning, I caught the train to Manchester. No other Americans were on the train. Nor were Americans roaming the streets in Manchester and spilling out of pubs and getting a wall job in every alley. I felt at one with the blokes.

But just as Irish Catholics can identify a Protestant a block away, blokes can identify an American. No matter how I dressed or how I tried to blend in, I was a stranger in a strange land.

The Victorian Gothic facade of the Rylands Library widened my eyes in amazement. It seemed more church than library. With more than a little diffidence, I walked inside, rooted my feet, and with an open mouth and wide eyes turned in a circle staring at the grand reading room, the stained-glass windows, and the statues of notable blokes.

I was wearing a windbreaker and khaki pants. But I felt underdressed in this cathedral of books. I roamed the stacks running my hands over titles, and avoided the central desk where a half dozen or so middle-aged women shuffled books and papers. I walked to the least intimidating of the women and stood before her. She looked at me with such surprise that I knew she did not see many Americans in this place. She was short and overweight, but her white hair, grandmother-like manner, and the white lace around her neck gave her great dignity.

One eyebrow rose about a millimeter, which is about as much curiosity as a bloke will allow, and asked, "May I be of assistance . . . sir?"

I leaned toward her and in a low voice asked, "Do you have a copy of the *Kama Sutra*?"

The errant eyebrow rose another millimeter. I could see the surprise on her face and the question in her eyes: How does he know of that book? Then her eyebrow realigned as she had a revelation: he wants to see the illustrations.

I smiled. If this book was written hundreds of years ago by people who knew so much about sex that they wrote a book on the subject and illustrated it with colorful and detailed artwork, then she was damn right. I wanted to see the illustrations.

Say what you will about blokes, the older ones have impeccable manners. The little lady pointed to a nearby table and said, "If you will have a seat in the reading area, one of our librarians will bring you a copy." She paused. "We will provide you with gloves that you will wear while handling the book. You cannot remove the book from the table. Our copy is an old one and quite rare. We ask that you treat it with respect."

"Yes, ma'am."

Her eyes held mine for a moment, and her thoughts were clear. Here is a young American, a military person, almost certainly one from the other ranks and by definition crass and unlettered. He does not know this is a revered and scholarly book. He thinks it is a sex manual.

She was very wise.

The *Kama Sutra* is appreciated on two levels. It is a book for scholars of ancient Hindu writings. And it is filled with detailed illustrations of every possible sexual position one can imagine and many that one cannot imagine. In fact, some of the positions are for acrobats or by those who have had their spines surgically removed. And there are some positions that no human can perform; they are there for the amusement of the guys who wrote the book.

I thumbed through the text, found the illustrations, and for perhaps an hour slowly turned the pages, quite proud of myself for continuing my education.

7

PERHAPS it was my sense of failure at losing one of the best jobs in the air force that caused me to fall in with two young airmen who were perpetual losers. These guys were born shit birds; no-account Southerners who came out of poverty into the only job they could find. They were on a fast track to trouble.

If Mother had met them, she would have pulled me aside and said, "Robert, they are not your kind of people."

But if I became friends with them and drank with them, then I was the same as them. And that meant my jumped-up desire to be a writer was a desperate and futile effort to escape my lot in life.

Cowboy was from Arkansas and was a slouching hound dog of a man with a mouth too large for his face. He was called Cowboy because of his stretched-out, loping walk. His face was pockmarked, and when he talked, his lips became wet, and he appeared to be on the edge of drooling. He was one of those people who could step out of a shower, shave, and dress in pressed clothes and still look rumpled, disheveled, and unclean. He was incapable of looking anyone in the eye.

Memphis was from—surprise—Memphis. A guy about my height, he had tousled blond hair and a contagious smile. At his core, he was one of the emptiest people I have ever known. His eyes were flat and vacant. He was vicious in a pub fight because he was throwing punches before his opponent realized a fight was on. In a fight, he was relentless. He seemed to feel no pain, but he caused a lot of pain to others. Far bigger men gave him a wide berth.

My friendship with these two men would introduce me to the windy side of the law and show me how very easy it is for a young man to make decisions that will change his life forever.

Even a half century later, my experience with these two men causes me discomfort. So I will go through it in a clean and quick manner. But I tell you straight up that the trouble to come was of my own making. I was not a victim.

It started the way most Saturday mornings started: Cowboy, Memphis, and I in the enlisted club knocking down can after can of beer. The room was cavernous. Most of the tables were empty. Enlisted men walked back and forth. The smell of beer filled the air. By noon we were drunk and so broke we knew we would not be going into Warrington. This Saturday we would have to stay on base and nurse the diluted beer in the enlisted club. We began hatching moneymaking schemes.

Cowboy leaned across the table and planted the seed. "I work over across the base in that there warehouse what stores furniture. That furniture is for the officers' club and the BOQ. Why don't we borrow some of that furniture and sell it? Nobody will know the difference." He leaned back and grinned, pleased with himself. "I got a key to the warehouse," he added. His lips glistened, and I didn't know if it was from beer or from his natural slobber.

Memphis narrowed his eyes. "What kind of furniture?"

"Fuck. Furniture. You know. Chairs, lamps, the sort of shit officers want in their rooms. That warehouse is big. I mean big. We could borrow a truckload, and nobody would ever know."

"Borrow?" I asked.

"He means steal it," Memphis said. That must have been pretty funny because Memphis and Cowboy leaned back and laughed.

"They got beer in there, too," Cowboy said. "All stacked up in a locked room."

"You got the key to that room, too?" Memphis asked.

Cowboy grinned, reached into his pocket, pulled it out, and waved it. "I got the key."

At that point, we were three bullshitting drunks; thinking out loud, blue-skying, nothing serious. We each took a long slow pull of beer. "We can't sell that stuff on base," I said. "Where would we sell it?"

My words were slurred. But Cowboy and Memphis were Southerners. They understood.

Cowboy said, "Blokes will buy anything made in the US of A. There'd be no trouble selling the furniture. Maybe we should take it to Liverpool."

"Rough town," I said.

Memphis puffed up like an angry cat. "Fuck rough. Let's take it to Liverpool."

Cowboy slumped over the table and said we had a big problem. How were we going to get the furniture off base? We could not carry the furniture through the main gate, and even if we did, we could not take it on the train. He paused a long moment and said carrying the furniture would be even more difficult if he also borrowed a case of beer.

For a moment, we were quiet. Despair hung in the air like an English fog. If I had said nothing, our plot would have gone no further. It would all have been empty talk, nothing but three young rednecks dreaming of a way to escape their lot in life.

But I broke the silence. I don't know if I did it to solve a problem, to impress my friends, or if a deep-seated character flaw was pulling me toward destruction.

"I can check out vehicles from the motor pool," I said.

Memphis smirked. Cowboy drooled, was quiet for a moment, and then said, "Get serious, or shut the hell up."

I announced that I'd earned my military driver's license when I was at Brize Norton and that it was good on any air force base in England. Cowboy rubbed his cratered face. He was trying to decide if what I said was even worth a response. Memphis wrinkled his brow and stared. At some feral level, he realized I was not joking.

"And . . . I got an off-base license."

Now both Memphis and Cowboy snorted in disbelief. Off-base licenses were for senior sergeants and officers. "Show it to me," Cowboy demanded.

I pulled out my wallet, found the license, and panned it in front of their disbelieving faces.

"Let me see that," Memphis said, jerking the license from my hand. He stared at the license, turned it over, stared, and then looked up with a wide grin. "Boys . . . we in business."

"We got to make a plan," Cowboy said. "We just can't jump in a truck and take off."

I said the first thing we had to do was put on fatigues over our civilian clothes. You can't be in an air force vehicle wearing civvies.

An hour later, I had checked out a pickup truck with a covered bed and loaded a wingback chair, two lamps, and a case of beer. How we got through the main gate, I do not know. Cowboy and Memphis stared straight ahead as I slowed, held my off-base license out the window, and the bored air policeman waved us on.

Once we were beyond the base, we whooped and clapped and opened more beer. I was too drunk to remember much about the trip. But I do remember that I was driving fast and having difficulty controlling the truck. And I remember seeing a queue of perhaps ten people at a bus stop, swerving off the road, and running down the curb at high speed, scattering blokes like a covey of quail. This did nothing to improve America's relations with Britain. And it was by the grace of God that I did not kill someone.

"Think they know who we are?" Cowboy shouted. A silly question, given that the truck was dark blue and had *US Air Force* painted on the doors.

"Where we gonna sell this shit?" I asked as we entered the outskirts of Liverpool.

"Go down to the docks," Memphis said. "Somebody there will buy it. Just find a parking space, and I'll sell it to the first bloke I see. We should get maybe twenty pounds. That's a nice chair."

"Take whatever you are offered," I said. "We can't go lollygagging all over Liverpool trying to sell furniture out of an air force vehicle."

We followed signs to the docks, driving slowly, and then I could smell the river and see ships tied up to docks with tall loading cranes hovering over them. Off to the side was a large and well-kept building. I wheeled into the parking lot, opened the door, and fell out of the truck, landed on my back, and cackled as empty beer cans clattered to the ground.

Cowboy and Memphis jumped out and came around the front of the truck laughing.

"What are you doing down there?" Cowboy asked. His voice trailed off.

I twisted and looked over my shoulder and saw a bobby—a British policeman. He was a big imposing bloke, and he wore a tin pot helmet on his head, which made him seem even bigger. Over his shoulder, I saw a sign that identified the nearby building as a police station. I had driven into the parking lot of a police station and was sprawled on the ground surrounded by beer cans.

"A bobby station," I said. "I don't believe this shit."

"You lot," the bobby said. "Where are you from, and what are you doing here?"

His voice was stern and as loud and as direct as that of a sergeant. Instinctively, we three jumped to our feet, lined up before the bobby, and stood at an approximation of attention. Well, we were weaving back and forth, but we thought we were at attention.

The bobby looked at the beer cans, at the civilian clothes visible under the fatigues, and stepped closer.

"I asked, 'Where are you from?'" he said.

I took one step forward, kept my eyes straight ahead, and said, "Sir, we are from RAF Burtonwood, and we are on a classified mission for the US Air Force."

The bobby's face remained impassive. "Right," he said. "And what might you have in that little lorry?"

"That ain't no lorry," Cowboy mumbled. "That's a truck."

"Sir, that's classified," I said.

Cowboy and Memphis giggled.

Another bobby came out of nowhere, went to the back of the truck, and pulled aside the canvas.

The first bobby spoke. "And where would you be taking this classified cargo?"

"To the docks, sir. To a boat."

"And the name of the vessel?"

"Sir, that's classified."

Cowboy and Memphis giggled again. By now, the bobbies realized that not only had they captured three drunks, but also they had broken up an international smuggling ring. The first bobby said, "You lot come inside while I call your air police." The second bobby moved in closer.

"Yes, sir," I said. The three of us turned and marched into the police station and into an open cell. The bobby shut the door behind us and shook his head in disbelief.

The air police hauled us back to Burtonwood and threw us into the stockade until our hearing. The next day, I was charged with misuse of a government vehicle, and the three of us were charged with misappropriation of government property. We were released from the stockade but told we were confined to base until a general court-martial convened in several months.

It began to register with me that I was in serious trouble. I'd grown up doing stupid things and being punished by my daddy. Many times, many, many times, he told me I was sorry and that I would never amount to anything. And then he would punish me for whatever I had done. The punishment was a beating administered with a belt or with a peach tree limb. I was familiar with the cycle. Now the air force was going to punish me. A general court-martial is the highest type of court-martial and can result in long-term stockade time.

I came from a military family. An ancestor, Sergeant William Coram, was George Washington's bodyguard during the Revolutionary War. In every war since then, the men of my family have gone to war. Five generations are buried in a remote country cemetery in southwest Georgia, and on many of those graves, the tombstone tells what branch of the service the men served in. Now I was about to bring shame upon my family name. I believed what Daddy had always told me, and I was determined to prove him right.

My way of handling the shame was to start drinking. I drank until it took great effort to stand erect. I was in the squadron recreation room shooting pool. I was ripping up furrows of green felt and laughing about it. My opponent grimaced in disgust, laid his cue on the table, and walked out. The other airmen in the room shook their heads and distanced themselves.

The first sergeant walked in, his presence dominating the recreation room. He saw what was going on and took charge. Using his sergeant's voice, he said, "Airman, get out of this recreation room and consider yourself confined to quarters until further notice."

I backed up when I heard his loud commanding voice. I looked at the stripes on his uniform and saw the same stripes my daddy had worn. I listened to the same loud, demanding voice, and I snapped. I had had enough of men shouting at me and giving me orders. I broke the cue stick on the edge of the table, picked up the heavy end, and stalked across the room toward the first sergeant. "You fucker. I'm going to kill you," I said.

This was the first time in my life I had ever threatened anyone. I am not a big guy, and while my judgment may be questioned in many things, I usually know better than to pick fights.

A first sergeant does not back up from an airman basic. He stood there. Another airman stepped in front of the first sergeant, held up his hands toward me, and in a placating voice said, "Cool down. Cool down." I am sure it was to save me from even more serious trouble.

"I'll kill you first," I shouted as I drew back the cue stick.

The airman looked into my crazed eyes, decided discretion was called for, and ran for the door. I followed, screaming, chasing him across the lawn and the road, all the while waving the cue stick.

The air policemen arrived, took away my cue stick, and put me in the stockade, where I would stay until the court-martial convened in two months. "Pretrial detention," they called it.

The young air force lawyer assigned to defend Cowboy and Memphis and me was a lieutenant in the Judge Advocate General's office, and his superiors thought representing three miscreants would be good experience. He thought we were from a lower social order, that we lacked brains, judgment, and common sense.

He may have been onto something.

"The evidence against you is strong and clear cut," he said. "About the only thing that can help you is character references from people in your hometowns."

From his face and voice, it was clear he thought the idea of any-one giving us a character reference was somewhere south of slim.

He was right about Cowboy and Memphis. But my mother went to the people of Edison and embarrassed herself by telling them I was in trouble and needed their help. She sent more than a dozen character references from the most prominent people in town. Even though I had no affection for my hometown, I had to admit that they took care of their own.

My young lawyer sighed. "Neither of your friends has a single reference. If I separated you from them, said you were unduly influenced, I think I can get you a much lighter sentence."

Maybe it was misplaced loyalty. Maybe it was reluctance to be put in a position that indicated I was better than my friends. I don't know. But I said, "No, sir. We did it together. We will be tried together."

Of course, the general court-martial found us guilty. We were sentenced to six months in the stockade.

8

Because I'd served two months of pretrial detention and was a good boy, I was released three months after I was sentenced. I said goodbye to Cowboy and Memphis, my fellow shit birds, and told them I would be waiting when they got out.

As I went through the release paperwork, the sergeant handed me several letters that had arrived during the months of my confinement. I remember two. One was from my sister, who said Mother had married the bookkeeper at the Chevrolet dealership. The second was from the jeweler in Washington, who had sent me the gold heart inscribed with *mizpah*.

The Friday I was released was almost six months to the day since I had arrived in Burtonwood from Brize Norton. Because I liked to stay in touch with my irrational side, I decided to go to Brize Norton and see Sarah. I wanted to explain why I'd broken our last date and why I'd left without saying goodbye.

Five months of back pay, even for an airman slick sleeve, was—at least for me—a lot of money. Early Saturday morning, I hired a taxi to take me to Brize Norton. I had no suitcase, no change of clothes, not even a toothbrush. I lit out for the territory some hundred and fifty miles away. The bloke cab driver and I did not speak during the five-hour ride. No doubt he was thinking of his fee, and

I suspect he was glad—at least for those hours—that Americans were stationed in England.

I was almost certain Sarah had found a new boyfriend by now. She was beautiful and lived near the main gate of Brize Norton where thousands of young Americans were stationed.

I stepped out of the cab, paid the driver, and stood on the street, looking up at the house where Sarah lived. I must have been there fifteen minutes before someone from inside saw me. A second-story window flew open, and there she was, smiling and waving.

"Where have you been?" she said. "You disappeared, and no one would tell me where you were. I tried so hard to . . ."

I waved for her to come down. "I'll tell you all about it. Want to go for a walk?"

Her smile widened. She disappeared. Seconds later, the front door flew open, and there she was, wearing a pair of white shorts and a sleeveless green blouse, her red hair blazing in the sunlight. In the open door behind her was her mother, wringing her hands. She was not happy that her daughter was running off with a Yank. But it was midafternoon, the sun was shining, and everyone knew Yanks were night creatures. What could happen on a warm, cloudless day, a day of the sort so rarely seen in England?

"We have to hurry," Sarah said. She seized my hand and pulled me down the street. "Me dad could come home any time, and he doesn't want me talking with Americans."

We walked behind her house, climbed a low stone fence, and half ran across a big pasture, over a hill, and down the back slope. We both were breathing hard. We stopped and looked around and saw the forest ahead of us. We turned, and the hill was behind us. We were isolated, out of sight of the world, and it was a beautiful sunny day. I turned, and she was in my arms. We sank to the knee-high grass, and now we were in a green cocoon and topped with a cloudless sky.

After a while, thinking of that pub on the banks of the Thames, I said, "I'll get us a room for tonight."

She paused for a long moment, too long, kissed me on the neck, and murmured, "I have a date tonight." Another pause. "He has a car."

I said I had to leave for Burtonwood Sunday and could she break her date. She raised on an elbow, kissed me, looked into my eyes, and said, "I'm going to marry him. He has a good job. Even me dad likes him." She kissed me again and said, "I hope you understand. Now tell me about Burtonwood and how you came to be up there so far away. You Yanks do move about."

I sighed and said it was a long story and perhaps I should leave now. She did not speak for a moment, and when she did, her voice changed. The warmth and the affection and the excitement were gone. In her heart, she had said goodbye to me and made a new and complete commitment to the bloke she was going to marry. "Well . . . if you want to leave."

In her voice was sadness for what might have been. For a chance to go to America.

For me, this was one more instance of being abandoned by someone I thought I cared about. I was getting used to this. Well, not really. I knew I would not be giving Sarah the *mizpah* jewelry.

A final hug, and then I turned and walked a half mile to a pub, where I called a taxi for the ride back to Burtonwood.

I don't like trains or buses or other forms of public transportation. In a taxi, I don't have to listen to the noises other people make or see their peculiar habits or smell their peculiar smells. When traveling, alone is better. When I threw the *mizpah* necklace out the window, there was no one to ask me why.

At the main gate at Burtonwood, I paid the driver and took a look at the money in my hand. Not much remained. But I had enough to go into Warrington and find a girl in a pub, a girl who wanted to fuck her way to America. I did not have enough money for a room. And I just wasn't in the mood for a knee-trembling wall job. When I asked a girl if she wanted to go back to the base, she agreed. Being on an American air base was a step closer to being in America.

We rode a bus to the base, and there we sneaked between buildings until we came to my Quonset hut. I say mine, but fourteen guys lived in there. It was Saturday night, so most of my fellow airmen were gone. But two guys were in their bunks. I glanced at them as the love of my life undressed and crawled into my single bunk.

I should have taken a closer look at the two other men in their bunks. One was the son of a bitch I had chased halfway across the base with a cue stick. I never noticed when he slipped out and reported me, and about twenty minutes later, an air policeman was standing on each side of my bunk. One of them was tapping me on the butt with his billy club and telling me to put on my clothes; they were taking me to the provost marshal's office to charge me with unlawfully having a female in my living quarters.

"It's illegal to have my girl in here?" I asked in surprise.

"You know it is," the AP said. "Put on your pants." He turned to my girl and said, "We will escort you to the main gate."

She was panic-stricken. The APs were big guys with helmets and shiny black belts, and they held billy clubs. She had to dress under the covers because the AP would not turn away.

The provost martial decreed that on Monday morning, I would stand before a summary court-martial. A summary court-martial is the baby of court-martials, sort of like traffic court, except the presiding officer can pass out a sentence up to thirty days. It is a balanced and fair process. A junior officer—he doesn't have to be a lawyer—hears the charges, finds the miscreant guilty, and sentences him for the maximum.

Monday morning, I reported to my squadron commander, a young and intense captain with his first command. He had no experience conducting courts-martial and shuffled the papers on his desk, looked at me, shuffled papers, looked at me. A particular paper caught his eye. He pulled it out of the pile and leaned back to read it again. When he looked at me again, his face was a question mark.

"You were released from the stockade Friday?"

"Yes, sir."

"And you are before me on Monday?"

"Yes, sir."

He sentenced me to thirty days, which I thought was a bit of overkill. And about five minutes after walking into the captain's office, I walked out . . . accompanied by an air policeman. At the stockade, Memphis and Cowboy asked if I'd had a good weekend.

AGAIN, I was a model prisoner and was released three weeks later. That night I went into Warrington and persuaded a girl to return to base with me. I don't think we were in the bunk five minutes before that same air policeman was tapping me on the butt with his billy club. He shook his head in disbelief as he frog-walked me out to his jeep. He said I must be from the South because I was so stupid.

I almost said, "So's your mama," but he had a billy club, and the guards at the stockade were his friends. Beyond that, there was some merit to his argument. I knew when I brought a bloke back to the barracks that, if caught, I would be court-martialed. Yet I did it. And when I was sentenced to the stockade, I expected it. My self-destructive behavior was one way to thumb my nose at my dead father.

The next morning, I again stood before the young squadron commander. He was surer of himself this time. He asked me how I pleaded to the charge. I said guilty. He said, "Thirty days." It was a brief encounter.

In the stockade, Memphis and Cowboy asked if I preferred the stockade to living in a Quonset hut. Because I was so experienced at this stockade business, I was the drill master for the several dozen men in the stockade. We drilled for hours every day in the tight confines inside the fence. I stood in the center of the drill area and had my charges following every command in the book. None of this straight-ahead stuff and column right for me. I marched them right up to the fence before I said, "To the rear, march." I had them doing left obliques and right obliques. They were always changing course, and the guards were impressed at how well they marched.

The day I was released, two APs met me at the gate and drove me to the squadron commander's office.

The young captain was gaining confidence and quickly took charge. He made me stand at attention, stared at me a moment, then he launched a most un-officer rant. "Airman, you have been court-martialed three times. You bring discredit to this squadron and to me."

He paused to study me a moment. "You have a young and innocent face and a very disarming manner. But you are nothing but trouble." He leaned across the desk, put on his serious face, and said, "The next time you are brought up on charges, any charges, I will see that you receive a long sentence followed by a bad conduct discharge." He stared. "We both know you will be back in here."

A BCD. That is serious shit. One step above below a dishonorable discharge. A BCD will hang around your neck the rest of your life. Nothing but menial jobs will be available. In the civilian world, the recipient of a BCD is a pariah.

The captain paused, held his ballpoint pen between two fingers, and rocked it back and forth on the desk, making a staccato noise. "You can avoid that," he said. "You can avoid some serious jail time by accepting a 39-17, an undesirable discharge."

He looked at me.

"Sir, I don't know what that is."

He said an undesirable discharge was somewhere between a general discharge and a bad conduct discharge: an administrative discharge.

I still did not understand. The captain helped me out. "It is not a good thing. But it is better than a BCD. And you will return immediately to CONUS."

CONUS is military speak for the continental United States.

I accepted his generous officer, and a few days later, I was escorted to Southampton. I did not understand why I needed an escort. My escort was a young sergeant who sat across from me on the train, his eyes never leaving me. He was half afraid that I might attack him, jump off the train, and remain in Bloke Land. He stayed with me until I climbed up the ramp of the troop ship.

I had served three years of what was to have been a four-year enlistment, and contrary to what the sarge always said, the military did not straighten me out. Although I made light of having an undesirable discharge, I was embarrassed and humiliated. My family would know I had broken the faith.

But I put on a good face. I had worn the uniform and done my bit toward pleasing the sarge. All of that was out of the way. Now I was a free man. Now I could concentrate on being a writer.

9

A boy becomes a man at twenty-one, often a promising young man. At twenty-one, a man's life is full of promise and hope, and he has an awareness the best is yet to come. A twenty-one-year-old man is a proud young man. And his parents are proud of him as he moves up in the world. But I was twenty-one, had flunked out of college, and been tossed out of the military. I could not go home and face my mother. For most of her life, she had been a military wife. She would be unforgiving about my being kicked out of the military. And the sarge? I did not want to think of what his reaction would have been had he been alive.

When the troopship docked in New Jersey, I went through the mustering-out process and was handed a copy of my undesirable discharge. Three men from my squadron back at Burtonwood were on the boat and were honorably discharged and going back home to get a job and begin their lives. My prospects were different.

One of my friends was Joe, a big, rangy guy from Chula Vista, California, who used his savings to buy a ten-year-old Chevrolet. He offered three of us a ride to wherever we were going. We had no route and no timetable. We were seeing America for the first time in years. We dropped off one guy in St. Louis, another in Denver.

Joe knew my turmoil and suggested I go to California with him and stay with his parents for a few weeks.

Joe's parents lived in a small sensible house in a lower-middle-class suburb. Joe was their only child, and now he was home from three years in England, and he brought a Southerner with him. His parents were not overjoyed. They wanted to celebrate Joe's return and did not want me involved in every conversation. But I was Joe's friend, and they tried to make the best of a situation that was uncomfortable for us all.

The day we arrived, I went to my room and was unpacking. Joe went to a nearby defense contractor and was offered a high-paying job. He had not been home more than an hour.

Joe's parents told me I could stay with them as long as I wanted. But I knew they were being courteous. Joe's dad introduced me to the owner of a service station, and the next day I was pumping gas. That night, Joe's mom asked me if I would mind paying a small rent for my room and meals. My salary at the gas station would not allow me to rent an apartment or buy a car.

Dinners were awkward. Joe talked of working on building jet aircraft, and I talked of how many cars I had filled with gas. I envied Joe when I saw the faces of his parents and they talked to him. When they turned to me, they were uncomfortable. They wanted me gone. And I wanted to be gone. But I had no place go.

For the first time in my life, I began reading the want ads in the newspaper. A couple of days later, I signed on for a job selling door-to-door magazine subscriptions. I bought a cheap gym bag, put in a couple changes of clothes, told Joe and his family goodbye, and moved into a motel with eight other young drifters, people who had not yet figured out what they wanted to do with their lives. We would all sell magazine subscriptions and make a little money while we waited for whatever life threw at us.

The boss was a dark and handsome guy in his midthirties. He had an edgy air about him and exuded a sense of latent violence. His crew chief was a big, muscular, middle-aged guy who had one facial expression: a scowl.

Each morning the boss and crew chief drove us salespeople to a subdivision and dropped us at the entrance. The homes were big and well-maintained and had trimmed lawns. To me, they were magnificent. It seemed that everyone in southern California was rich.

We salesmen were on our own with many doorbells to ring. Bathroom stops and lunch, we had to figure out. I grew used to entering a house and—in the middle of my memorized sales pitch—stopping to ask if I might use the bathroom. People in southern California were good about letting strangers use their bathrooms.

In my first week, I sold dozens of subscriptions but got only a few dollars in return. The boss said the big payoff was at the end of the month. He held us in bondage by withholding most of our commission, knowing that few of us would hang around for a month.

I heard the crew manager tell the boss, "That Southern kid can be one of the best we got if he stays with us."

But I didn't stay. I wanted to write for magazines, not sell subscriptions to magazines. I had to go home. I had to face Mother. I had to get a job and return to college. I had to get on with being a writer.

The next morning, I looked in my wallet and counted seven dollars. I told the crew chief I was leaving and wanted my back pay. The crew chief said I was leaving before payday, and he was not going to pay me a dime. And since I was leaving, I should pack my bag right now, talk to none of the other crew members, and meet him at his car in five minutes. He would drive me to the nearest expressway entry ramp. Any crew member who left was a bad seed that had to be uprooted and cast to the winds.

I stood on the expressway for about two hours and caught a ride to Anaheim, about a hundred miles north. About two minutes after I got out of the car, a California Highway Patrolman rolled up on his motorcycle, face impassive behind his dark sunglasses, booted the kickstand down, and said, "I need to see some identification."

As I pulled out my wallet, he said, "Where are you going?"

"Georgia."

"Georgia?"

"Yes, sir. Georgia."

He looked at my license and said, "You are going the wrong way."

I told him I had been discharged from the air force, gone to San Diego with a friend, and now was going home. He shook his head in a weary fashion, and his thoughts were written on his face: Georgia people are too dumb to find their way home.

He handed me my license, said it was illegal to hitchhike on California expressways, and that if I had not been a recently discharged veteran, he would arrest me for vagrancy. "Get off the expressway at the next exit," he said. "Take any road east."

I wonder if my going the wrong direction was an unconscious manifestation of my feelings about southwest Georgia. The landscape of my childhood was bitter and strewn with boulders. From that landscape, I had sustained many wounds, none life-threatening but all crippling and painful and everlasting.

Years later, a therapist would ask me if there were any times in my childhood that I felt safe. I flinched and, for a moment, was mute. And then I realized the only time in my childhood that I had felt safe was a summer I'd spent with my aunt and uncle on their remote farm. That summer I was free: free to spend all day in the woods, free to wear nothing but a pair of shorts and to follow my uncle as he plowed his cotton one row at a time behind a sway-backed and broken old mule, free to talk openly with my aunt and uncle, who loved me unconditionally. But most of all, I was free to read.

My aunt and uncle had a Bible and a novel by Frank Yerby called *The Foxes of Harrow*. I asked where the book came from, and they did not know. "It just showed up," my aunt said. I spent weeks reading that book. The backstory was how black people could be educated and polished and urbane but yet were held under the boots of whites who saw nothing but black skin. Frank Yerby said white people were incapable of believing that black people might not only be their equals but in many ways their superiors. The book changed my young life.

I grew up in a time and a place burdened with bone-deep racism. Frank Yerby had such an impact on me that when school resumed that September, I went to the library and asked if there were any books by Frank Yerby. The librarian thought I was a bit young to read such novels but gave me three books. None had dust jackets. I believe because people in southwest Georgia thought of books as they thought of oranges or bananas: you had to peel them to find the substance. Then a new book by Yerby arrived, and it had a dust jacket, and I saw that he was a black man from South Georgia: the first black man in America to write best-sellers. He was a millionaire. I held that book in my hand for long minutes, staring at Mr. Yerby's face and again and again reading his brief biography. A year later, I read that Mr. Yerby moved to Spain because of the racism in his home state. I was moved by his story and came to believe that if a black man in Georgia—with all the obstacles that implied—could write best-selling novels, maybe I, too, could one day write books. Frank Yerby became my hero.

Like him, I had no respect and no affection for my home state. When I eventually left Edison to go to college, the departure was more than going to another part of the state. The departure was my first step into a new world. And I knew that I would not, could not, ever return.

But now I was leaving California—or trying to leave California—and go home.

It was dark when I found myself in Riverside, a hundred miles from where I had begun that morning. To celebrate the speed of my journey, which was about half the pace of a Conestoga wagon, I went into a drugstore and spent my seven dollars on sunscreen and candy bars.

I was broke when I crossed the California state line into Arizona.

Today that ten-day hitchhiking trip across America is a blur, a series of disconnected anecdotes: the bitter cold of the desert during an October night, drinking beer in Arizona with Mexican copper mine workers, knocking on the front door of preachers' houses in small towns and trying to ignore the looks of pity and revulsion from their families when I asked for food or a few dollars.

One man gave me a ride of almost a thousand miles in his rattling old double-ended Studebaker. When mealtime approached, he would pull off the road at the city limits of the next town and let me out. While he ate his meal, I hiked through town, and he picked me up on the outskirts. I learned how to endure hunger. And I learned how to brave my shame when I drew curious looks in small towns across the west. More than one police chief stopped me and, after hearing my story, said, "Just keep on going, son. Nothing for you in this town but a vagrancy charge."

Going back home was running a gauntlet in which I faced fresh humiliation in every new place. Ten days after I left San Diego, I found myself in Fort Gaines, a small town on the Georgia-Alabama border about fifteen miles west of Edison. I had been to this town a hundred times as a boy, and I knew many residents. But I stood by the road until midafternoon, unable to get a ride for that last few miles. I kicked my toes in the red clay and looked east. Home was so close. Late that afternoon, I went to a farmhouse and asked if I could use the telephone. I didn't want to call for help. I wanted to walk up to the front door of the house where I had grown up, knock, and say I was home. But I had to ask Mother to come get me, to drive me the last few miles.

A half hour later, a new Chevrolet slowed as it approached, made a U-turn, and there was Mother sitting in the passenger seat. She rolled the window down and said, "Hello, son." No hug. No kiss on the cheek. Just hello. I leaned in the window and kissed her and noticed she was very pregnant.

Her husband, Frank, was around sixty years old, more than twenty years older than Mother. I guess she liked older men.

"Hello, Frank," I said.

Frank turned his head sideways, not enough to look me in the eye, and grunted. My stepfather did not like his oldest stepson. He did not like it that Mother's oldest son was moving in. I understood. My younger sister and brother were still at home. And Mother and Frank had a child on the way. It was a quiet ride home. I had no stories to tell. Frank had nothing to say. Mother had no news.

We pulled into the driveway of the house where I had spent my childhood. I jumped out and opened the door for Mother and held her arm as she struggled to get out of the car. Damn, she was big; great with child, as the Bible would say.

"When is the baby due?" I asked, figuring childbirth was a safe topic.

"A few months." Mother did not want to talk about the baby. She knew I had been kicked out of the military, and her eyes were filled with anguish as she looked at me. "Take your old room. We will talk later." She stopped and shook off my helping hand. "Son, you can stay as long as you want. This is your home. But I want you to get a job."

In an instant, I realized I was the subject of a lot of gossip in Edison. A dozen people had written character references for me. A stream of people had come into the office at the Chevrolet dealership, and some of them had asked Frank about me. As a bookkeeper, he had to keep everything neat and tidy and in good order. The books had to be balanced, and he wanted his life to be balanced. But I had thrown his life out of whack.

I nodded toward Frank, picked up my small gym bag, and started walking toward the house.

"Robert," Frank snapped.

I turned. "Yes, sir?"

"Get that job as soon as you can."

It was good to be home.

10

I was right. The story of my first court-martial had made the rounds in Edison. The current version was that I had stolen a truck in England and smuggled a load of something—no one was sure of what—to Turkey, was caught, and kicked out of the air force.

No one ever mentioned the English Channel and how I got the truck from England to the continent. But in the South, it is the story, not the facts, that matter. The story, no matter how far-fetched, becomes true in the telling. And saying I had smuggled a load of something to Turkey made a better story than saying I had smuggled furniture to Liverpool. Small Southern towns are shrouded in myth, friendliness, helping those who are down on their luck, and bringing food to every house struck by death. There is an element of truth in all of those. But those who live in small Southern towns like nothing more than jumping on people who have faltered. They revel in the misfortune of others.

Everyone in Edison knew of the sarge and his thirty years in the army. They knew that if he were still alive, I would not have dared to come home.

No one asked me direct questions about my time in England. Just tangential inquiries. My standard response was that it was good to be home after three years, but I wanted to find a job and get on with my life.

I had no car, and there were no jobs in Edison. Mother said, "Son, you need to get out of Edison." She called a cousin in Milledgeville, a small town about 160 miles northeast of Edison. The cousin owned a grocery store and was prosperous. "Send Robert on up here," he said. "We got plenty of room. I'll find something for him to do."

I rode the bus to Milledgeville—a ten-hour trip with a layover in Albany and another in Macon. My cousin, an overweight jovial fellow with a perpetual smile, met me at the bus station, threw my single piece of luggage into the trunk, said, "Let's go."

We were not out of the parking lot when he said, "Robert, now that you are out of the service, what do you want to do?"

After a long moment, I said, "I want to be a newspaper reporter, maybe write books."

My cousin nodded and did not speak for a long moment. It was the reaction he would have had if I had said I wanted to fly a rocket to the moon. He nodded and made a humming noise and said, "Well, we don't have any of those in Milledgeville. But if you want a good stable job, I'll get you on at the state hospital. You'll find plenty to write about out there."

What my cousin called the state hospital was Georgia's hospital for the insane. In Georgia, the asylum was known as *Milledgeville*, the name of the town synonymous for the mental institution. Telling someone, "You belong in Milledgeville," was the same as saying, "You are crazy as a shithouse rat."

Milledgeville was a place of medieval horror, a warehouse for God's mistakes. Some thirteen thousand patients were locked inside the bleak and foreboding buildings and attended by only forty-eight doctors. It was the largest mental institution in the world.

The hospital was controlled by a local state senator. My cousin owned the largest grocery store in town and was friends with the senator. He also contributed to the senator's reelection campaigns. My cousin called the senator, who said he would notify the hospital that I was coming to work there. I went to the hospital, and a junior administrator said, "We put you on the receiving ward as an attendant." There was no interview, and I had no choice of where in the hospital I wanted to work. The senator had said to put this guy to work, and that's what they did.

I told the administrator that I wanted to return to college and would be here only long enough to save a little money. He wasn't interested.

He said, "We have a few rooms on the receiving ward if you need a place to stay. Rent is free. Small room. Bath. No kitchen. But you can have your meals with the patients. A number of staff people do that."

So I packed my gym bag and went to the receiving ward to meet the head attendant, my boss. His name was Wilbur.

He was a middle-aged man whose face was as round as his stomach, so round that his eyes were recessed in wrinkles of fat and glinted with resentment at life. "College boy," he sneered at our first meeting. The administrator had told him I got the job because of political influence—which made me dangerous—and that I was going back to college—which made me even more dangerous.

"I hear you will be living on the ward," he said. He liked that because it meant I was available all hours of the night. My room was at the end of the hall closest to the locked doors that opened into the elevator bay. "Put your stuff in there," he said, handing me a key. "Then get on back down here, and I'll show you around, tell you about the hospital, and introduce you to everyone."

It never occurred to me that living on the floor with more than one hundred disturbed people was a bit unusual.

The center of the hospital was the administration building, a long, three-story building that stood perpendicular to the entrance gate. The receiving ward for men was on the second floor. Here was where every new patient came until he was diagnosed and moved to another building. We had a building for the incurably insane, a building for the criminally insane, a medical building, and a half dozen or so "back wards" that served as warehouses. Patients who went into the warehouse buildings were never released. The hospital was diagnostic and custodial, most often custodial, and the recovery rate for patients was too low to be measured.

The receiving ward was also home to alcoholics and drug abusers whom the courts sent to serve thirty days before being released, thirty days being considered long enough to dry out or to kick the habit. Most of the alcoholics and drug users had been here more than once and knew the hospital routine as well, if not better, than the attendants. Many were "help patients" and worked in clerical or custodial jobs. They were a jovial lot and required minimum care: a daily shot of B-12 and an occasional counseling session. Attendants were encouraged to sit in on these sessions, which were like conversations between old friends. The friends knew they would soon part. And they knew they would soon be reunited. It was something like my leaving the stockade and my friends, knowing I would soon return.

No doctor at the hospital was a psychiatrist. The two doctors on the receiving ward were former patients. One had been addicted to pills and was considered more or less cured. The other was a small, frail man with a skinny body that was twisted like an old apple tree. His history could not be discussed.

The nurses on the receiving ward were the normal people in the hospital, wise and dedicated women. And there was a nurse from the medical building who came through occasionally and was deferred to by everyone, including the two doctors. It was said she performed operations on patients, even hip surgery that staff doctors were reluctant to do. But she was a presence, and when she walked down the hall, all who encountered her stepped aside.

The other three attendants on the receiving ward had been there for years and enjoyed telling me what they had seen and heard in their time at Milledgeville. They liked to talk of the doctor who performed lobotomies. The attendants said a lobotomy was a simple procedure. The doctor forced an instrument, something like an ice pick, through the patient's temple, wiggled it a bit, and that was it. After performing a lobotomy, and he did dozens of them, he always turned to the nurses and attendants and said, "Anybody else want me to change their day?"

I was by several decades the youngest attendant on the ward. The other three were the same sort of Southerners you would find working on a farm, in a cotton gin, or being a clerk in a hardware store. None had any education in psychology or any training beyond what they picked up on the job. The lack of entrance requirements for attendants is best illustrated by the fact I was hired, and I knew jack shit about anything. I was marking time until I returned to college and became a newspaper reporter. The attendants were hard men with flat eyes and impassive faces; emotional flatliners untroubled by the chaos of the ward, men who had no compunction about entering the room of a noisy patient, beating him senseless, then walking away, believing they had done their jobs. Compassion was a foreign concept.

Dr. Hood was the most important and most respected doctor in the hospital. It did not matter that he had been a patient here a few years earlier. He was about five feet tall, and his large head was cast to his right side. To look at someone, he had to turn his body toward them. He walked on the tips of his toes with one shoulder elevated to around his ear. When he walked, his arms were outstretched, and his fingers were curved into claws. But his eyes were gentle, all-seeing and all-knowing. He was sincere when he welcomed me to the hospital. "Please come in anytime you want to talk," he said.

Wilbur touched me on the arm and motioned toward the door. He thanked Dr. Hood. As we walked down the hall, he motioned with his head back toward Dr. Hood's office. "Stroke. Smartest man in the hospital. Or just about anywhere else. Wrote all sorts of papers and books. Young doctors rotating through here treat him like he is famous. All the doctors consult with him about their difficult cases."

He snorted. "But he can't get a job anywhere else." He tilted his head toward me and whispered, "He was a dope fiend. Probably still is." He looked at me, and when he spoke, his voice was hard. "Forget what he said about his open door. Do your job. Anything else, you talk to me first."

Dr. Blake, the second doctor on the floor, was about twenty years younger than Dr. Hood but was the senior doctor on the floor. He was well-dressed, courtly, and a bit preoccupied. He had patrician features, and diplomas on his wall showed he had an undergraduate degree from Yale and a medical degree from Harvard.

"My door is always open," he said. "Come see me anytime." I sensed he was not sincere, that he was being courteous to a new attendant.

As Wilbur and I walked down the hall, he whispered, "Pillhead. He used to have a big practice in Atlanta but had to give it up. The courts agreed not to pull his license if he would work here for five years." He snorted again. "I could tell you some things about him."

The last staff person I met was the staff psychologist, a slight man in his early thirties who dressed with style and was the most flamboyant gay man I had ever seen. I don't remember his name. But I do remember that he flounced and he pranced and he giggled. He was genius smart. And his eyes were filled with more sadness than I had ever seen.

When we were introduced, he tilted his head and said, "You may have noticed that I display all the signs of being a homosexual." He looked at Wilbur, and his lips curled in a sardonic fashion. "What some people call a queer. Well, I am. That's why I'm here. I had a private practice in Atlanta but got beaten up just about every time I walked down the street. I began using . . . medication." He threw his hands wide. "And here I am."

He smiled and cocked his head. "The patients know I may be able to help them, and they are kind to me. So are the nurses." He looked at Wilbur. "I can't say that about everyone."

The head attendant smirked. He might be nothing more than an attendant, but he was not a queer. And he thought being a queer was even lower than being an attendant.

"But you seem different," the psychologist said. "Perhaps we can be friends. I need friends." He looked at me a long moment. "The head nurse said you had been to college and that you are going back and you want to be a newspaper reporter."

Wilbur snorted. He was standing between a queer and a would-be writer and couldn't decide which he most detested.

"Let's have dinner one night," the psychologist said. "I want to hear all about your plans."

"He's working nights for the first two weeks," Wilbur said. He turned and motioned for me to follow. We were but few steps away when he said loudly enough for the psychologist to hear, "He didn't tell you about the little boys they caught him with." He shook his head. "Homo."

Wilbur opened a locked door and handed me two pairs of blue scrubs. I realized that the hospital was not just a dumping ground for patients but one for doctors, staff, and other lost souls who had nowhere else to go. People like me.

Because I was young and wanted to go back to school, the nurses liked me. Unlike the other attendants, I had a future. And I amused the nurses. I was an anxious and unlettered small-town boy who wore pistol-legged pants and rolled up the sleeves of his short-sleeved shirts as far as they would go. I knew nothing about anything. But I had dreams. Perhaps my dreams were unrealistic, but I had dreams.

Being liked by the nurses, of course, made me even more disliked by my fellow attendants. And because I was the new guy, I had my share of unpleasant jobs: emptying bedpans, cleaning shit off the floor and walls—I never knew that some people liked to take a dump then pick it up and throw it at passersby.

My first months went well. Nurses and doctors said there was no better place to learn about the human condition than in a mental institution. Here I would find plenty of material to write about.

ONE day, I was walking down the hall and passed Dr. Hood's open door. He motioned me in. That was the beginning of almost daily conversations. We talked of college and religion and marriage and whatever was on his mind . . . or whatever he pulled from me that was on my mind. He was a gentle pile driver in his questions, and he was the first accomplished person who ever took a genuine interest in me.

I realized that, to compensate for the ravages to his body, his mind was a flaming torch that enabled him to see further into the darkness of the human condition than could most of his contemporaries. The beauty of his thought and the power of his intellect shone through, and I forgot what his body looked like.

One day we talked of religion, and I said I was troubled by the factual inconsistencies of the Bible; that I had too many questions that could not be answered.

He smiled. "And that bothers you?"

I nodded. "I was brought up in the church, but now all I have are questions."

"You would like for it to be otherwise?"

For reasons I did not understand, I was suddenly filled with emotion and could not speak. I nodded.

He smiled a gentle smile, nodded, and said something I would never forget: "Robert, religion is not an intellectual exercise. If you want to believe, then simply believe."

I stared, not understanding. This sounded too simple.

As if reading my mind, he said, "People like to make religion complicated. It is not. If you want to question every statement in the Bible and if you want to undertake a study of theology to prove the Bible wrong, that is fine. And it may be intellectually satisfying. But it will never lead you toward the solace and comfort I believe you seek." He paused, stared deep into my soul, then in a slow and distinct voice said, "If you want to believe, just believe."

11

IF Dr. Hood wanted to teach me theology, Wilbur wanted to teach me humility. I learned how to give an enema. I learned when to call for help when dealing with a disturbed patient. I learned how to give injections. I learned how to assist with shock treatment. I learned to be blasé about chronic masturbators. I learned that when a patient ran away, we did not say he had *escaped*; we said he had *eloped*. And I learned how upset Wilbur could be when I did not follow hospital protocols.

One afternoon after lunch, the phone rang in the closet-like room that was Wilbur's lair. He was nowhere in sight, so I walked inside answered his phone, listened, and said, "I'll be right down."

I took the elevator to the ground floor where two muscular state troopers stood beside their blue-and-gray cruiser. These guys were tense, elbows bowed, ready for anything. The troopers' uniforms were mussed, their faces were tight, and between them—shackles binding his hands and feet—was a new patient. He was about five feet eight inches tall, a brown complexion, and wiry. He had long unkempt black hair, was barefooted, and wore faded bib overalls. His eyes darted about, and he emitted a feral growl as his head swung back and forth like a cornered panther looking for a bolt hole.

One of the troopers handed me a folder containing the patient's records, looked at me, shook his head, and said, "You gonna need some help." I signed the transfer form and looked at the patient. His face was bruised.

"It took two of us to get him in the car and bring him down here," one trooper said. "He is bad news, and he is stouter than he looks." He paused. "He did not want to leave his house up in the mountains."

I looked at the patient. "You going to give me any trouble?" I asked.

My question did not register for a moment. And then his eyes softened. He did not know where he was, but he knew that I would not—could not—beat the hell out of him as had the troopers. Whoever I was and wherever he was could not be as bad as who he was and where he had been.

He shook his head, and with the distinctive sharp accent of the southern Appalachians, said, "No, Shorty. I won't give you no trouble."

"Take off his chains," I said to the trooper.

The big trooper shook his head. "I don't know about that."

"He is my patient now. Take off his chains."

To the patient, I said, "We are going upstairs. Everything will be fine."

As the trooper unlocked his chains, he said, "Will you stay with me, Shorty?" He was almost pleading.

"Every minute."

The trooper pulled the chains loose, stepped back, and waited, ready to wrestle the patient to the ground at the least sign of resistance. "He's all yours."

I looked at the top page of the patient's folder, found his name, and said, "Mr. Sikes, are you ready to go upstairs with me?"

The patient's expression told me it had been a long time since anyone had called him *Mister*. His shoulders loosened. He stood a bit straighter. "Okay, Shorty."

"Let's go." I turned, and he followed me.

Over my shoulder, the troopers stared in disbelief.

"We are going to get on the elevator and go up two floors. I will introduce you to the attendants and to your doctor. The doctor will help you and answer all your questions."

"Elevator?"

"Yes."

"I ain't never been on no elevator."

"It's okay. Takes a few seconds. I will be with you."

"You staying with me all the time?"

"As long as you want me to."

An agitated Wilbur was waiting when I stepped off the elevator. He looked at me, at the patient, backed up a step, and said, "You okay?"

Puzzled, I handed him the patient's folder and told him I was fine. Then I turned to the patient and introduced him to Wilbur. The patient sidled closer to me and mumbled, "Shorty."

I asked Wilbur if he wanted me to process the new patient. Wilbur was cautious and kept his eyes on the patient and said, "Go ahead. And then take him to Room Ten."

I looked at Wilbur. Room Ten was a padded room, locked at all times, and reserved for the most violent patients.

Wilbur saw I was about to ask him a question. "Go ahead," he snapped, motioning for me to go down the hall.

"Mr. Sikes, you ready?"

Mr. Sikes said if I stayed with him, he would go wherever I wanted.

Wilbur leaned closer. "Make sure you lock the door when you leave."

I did a quick bit of paperwork on Mr. Sikes, noticing that the nurses and other attendants were watching. What the hell was going on here? Why such interest in the new patient? I opened the door to Room Ten and led Wilbur inside.

"I have to go do a few things," I said. "I will be back in five minutes."

"Shorty, don't leave me."

I touched him on the shoulder and said, "I'm not leaving you. I just have to do a few things. I'll be back before you know I'm gone."

When I locked the door and turned around, Wilbur was waiting. He was so angry he was bouncing from one foot to the other. "I knew you were stupid, college boy, but until today I did not know just how stupid you are."

I thought I had done Wilbur a favor by meeting the new patient and checking him in. I stared, not knowing what I had done wrong.

Wilbur pointed at the door of Room Ten. "That patient you just put in there . . . that patient you went down by yourself to pick up, he killed his brother, broke a neighbor's leg, and when the sheriff came to arrest him, he put the sheriff in the hospital. It took three state troopers to put him in chains. He is a violent man. Very violent. And you went down by yourself to admit him. You are as crazy as he is. If something had touched him off, he could have cleaned out every attendant on this ward."

I chuckled and pointed toward the door of Room Ten. "That guy? You must have him mixed up with someone else. You saw how easy he came with me."

Wilbur interrupted. "And why in the hell didn't you notify me? Two or three of us could have brought him up. Whatever made you do that by yourself?"

Now I was getting angry. "Your phone rang, and you were not there to answer it. So I answered it. The operator said a patient was downstairs. That's all she said. I thought I was doing my job."

"Well, a minute after you left, the operator called back and gave the nurse his history and said we should send three attendants to admit him."

"No wonder the troopers . . ."

Wilbur, muttering to himself, turned and headed toward the nurses' station. I passed a few minutes later and heard the chief nurse say, "You mean Robert brought him up here all by himself?"

THE first time Mr. Sikes was taken out of his room to see Dr. Blake, he fought three attendants so hard they backed out of the room. All the time, Mr. Sikes was shouting, "Where is Shorty?"

The three attendants leaned against the wall, breathing hard. I opened the door and said, "Mr. Sikes, may I take you to see your doctor? You will like him."

"Shorty, where you been? I don't like those people."

"I need you to go with me to see your doctor."

"You will stay with me?"

"I will. I will sit with you while you talk with the doctor."

He followed me out of the door and down the hall, ignoring the three attendants. Dr. Blake was annoyed when Mr. Sikes insisted I stay during the first interview. But he had read Mr. Sikes's record, knew I had admitted Mr. Sikes, and he agreed. During that interview, and all subsequent interviews Mr. Sikes had with the doctor, he would not go unless I accompanied him. And during the interviews, he would on occasion turn to me and say, "Shorty, I don't know if I want to talk to him about that."

I told him it was okay to talk with the doctor about anything, that the doctor wanted to help him.

A few days later, the three attendants made another attempt to move Mr. Sikes. That visit ended with Mr. Sikes still in his room and one of the attendants going to the medical ward.

Afterward, I would be walking down the hall, and Mr. Sikes would see me through the small window in the door and bang for my attention. I often unlocked the door, went inside, and talked with him. And I accompanied Mr. Sikes every time he left his padded room. I insisted he not wear a straitjacket. As we walked down the hall, we chatted like old friends, and he never gave me a moment's trouble.

The head attendant never forgave me.

Mr. Sikes received numerous injections of Thorazine, a powerful tranquilizer. I began accompanying him to receive shock treatment. There was no informed consent, and many new patients were routinely given shock treatments before being transferred to the back wards. Shock treatment caused a loss of cognition and amnesia. Or, as Wilbur said, "It quiets them down." I assisted with perhaps a half-dozen shock treatments for Mr. Sikes. I helped him up on the gurney, strapped him down, put the padded tongue depressor in his mouth, and told him to bite down on it. I talked to him during the entire process as the nurses continued with the prep, gave him an injection of a curare derivative to relax him, and I held his hand until the doctor motioned for me to step away from the gurney. The doctor flipped a switch, and Mr. Sikes's trembling body arced until nothing but his heels and the back of his head touched the gurney. His eyes rolled back in his head, and he was unconscious.

Wilbur was right. The treatments quieted Mr. Sikes down. On the day he was transferred to a back ward, he did not recognize me.

A few days later, an elderly patient had an impacted bowel, a common problem with drug users. Wilbur gave me a set of rubber gloves and a tongue depressor and said, "Okay, college boy. Dig it out."

It took twenty minutes. But piece by piece, I dug out about a pound of rock-hard old-man shit from the patient's flabby ass. He thanked me.

By living on the ward and taking my meals with the staff, I soon saved enough money to make a down payment on a ten-year-old Mercury. Never mind that I had to add a quart of oil every time I filled the gas tank, and never mind that when I drove down the highway, I left a trail of blue smoke; this was my first car, and I felt the pride and freedom that every young man feels when he has a set of car keys in his pocket.

All was going well. I figured in another six months I would have saved enough money to move to Atlanta, get a job, and enroll in college. I was more than a little pleased at how I had bounced back after the failures in my past. But always there was hanging over me the fact I had an undesirable discharge. And I knew that when I went to Atlanta to find a job, I would have to go to employers who hired college students and did not ask detailed background questions.

I had a dim sense that the time at the state hospital was an important hinge in my life; that I was negotiating that space between what I had been and what I was to become. I was more excited about my prospects than at any other time in my young life.

And then came a series of events that changed everything.

12

ONE morning after breakfast, I went to the break room and found nurses reading the *Atlanta Constitution*. I heard a lot of exclamations like "I know that doctor" and "How did he find *that* out?" and "Oh, my Lord." One of the nurses looked up and whispered, "What are the doctors saying?" She told me to look down the hall and tell her what the doctors were doing. I peered around the corner and saw Dr. Blake striding toward Dr. Hood's office, newspaper in hand. "They are having a powwow," I said. "What's going on?"

"Read this," the nurse said, moving the paper so I could look over her shoulder. On the front page was a story by a reporter named Jack Nelson who wrote about what he called "medieval conditions" at the hospital, the nurse who performed hip surgery, and about shock treatments given to calm patients down before they were sent to one of the back wards.

I laughed.

The heard nurse twisted around, eyes narrowed, and demanded, "What are you laughing about?"

I shrugged. "When I was growing up, this paper made my daddy mad every morning he read it. He would crunch the newspaper and throw it across the room." I shrugged. "I guess the paper still has that effect on people."

In a rare moment of discretion, I did not add that it was stories like this, and reactions like this, that made me want to become a newspaper reporter. The nurse turned back to the paper. "I would give anything to know what the superintendent is doing."

Shitting a brick, I thought.

"Look," I said, pointing to the bottom of the story. A note in italics said this was the first in a series of articles the paper would be running about the state hospital. The nurse sighed, whispered, "Dear God," folded the paper, and placed it on the table.

In the 1950s and 1960s, and even into the middle 1970s, newspapers had a power that today is unimaginable. Newspapers were the only medium that mattered. The power of radio was fading, and television was perpetual amateur hour. When people wanted news, they picked up a newspaper. They believed the paper. They trusted the paper.

Few papers dominated a region as much as the Atlanta newspapers dominated the South. The Atlanta papers could make or break almost any politician. In the Atlanta area, the papers were a mighty force, hated and feared by politicians and rascals. The secret fear of every elected scoundrel in the state was that a reporter from Atlanta might knock on his door.

Both John Pennington on the *Journal* and Jack Nelson on the *Constitution* wreaked hell, chaos, and destruction on corrupt city, county, and state government, along with gambling dens, state prisons, and just about anything that struck their attention.

John Pennington had just done a series about the infamous Buford Rock Quarry, a prison camp in north Georgia where inmates spent their days at hard labor, a place where guards beat and even killed prisoners. With each part of the series was a small picture of what Pennington had found scratched on the wall of a cell, a wail of despair that said, "They Is No God."

Nelson and Pennington were avenging angels who were loved by the afflicted and loathed by the comfortable. They started fires, and they put out fires. These reporters, at a time when no one else could do this, made people believe the guilty could be caught and held accountable.

These reporters were the last of their kind. Sometime in the mid-1970s, there would come a sea change in the news business. The time was different in each local market but depended on when, for the first time, a television station broke a big story and owned it. On the national level, there is disagreement about what story brought television into the ascendancy. Some say it was the first manned moon shot in 1969. Others say it was the early and mid-1970s when television brought the Vietnam War into living rooms across America. But there is no argument that television became the dominant medium and the influence of newspapers lessened. Some newspaper reporters became "content providers" or "multiplatform journalists." Computers became more important than shoe leather. And once again, the era of knights and crusades ended and the world became a lesser place.

But in 1959, Jack Nelson had unleashed the outrage of the *Constitution* upon my employer, a state institution long overlooked by the public. The hospital was a place whose name was whispered, a place of shame.

For the next few days, doctors held meetings behind closed doors. Tension oozed down to the nurses and staff.

Nelson was relentless, a new story almost every day: one about staff doctors who were former patients, another about doctors with a history of alcohol or drug abuse, and still another about a doctor in a back ward who used experimental drugs on hopeless patients.

We all knew that Nelson had a source inside the hospital. But that source did not work on the receiving ward because Nelson never wrote anything about our doctors or staff or conditions. A great gulf existed between the receiving ward and the other wards. The receiving ward was where new patients went until they were diagnosed and began a treatment regimen. After they had been numbed by shock treatments or rendered into pale robotic figures by a lobotomy, they were warehoused until they died. Often their families did not claim their bodies, and one more unmarked grave was added to the hospital cemetery. It was a cemetery of the forgotten. A potter's field.

With each of Nelson's stories, tension grew in the hospital. And the hospital superintendent reacted in the usual way of corrupt Georgia officials. He told Nelson, "You work for that lying, Communist-loving, nigger-loving *Atlanta Constitution*." Nelson quoted him on the front page.

The superintendent, in his overweening arrogance and godlike status at the hospital, forgot he was talking to a man whose employer bought ink by the barrel. Or if he remembered, he was so secure in his position that he did not care.

One night, Nelson went out for dinner at a Milledgeville restaurant, and a doctor slugged him for dragging the name of the hospital through the mud. Nelson was a former Golden Gloves boxing champion, but that night he did not defend himself. I sensed that, by not hitting the doctor, Nelson had kept above the roiling personalities, that he was just doing his job.

One morning, I glanced out the window and saw a white car ease down the driveway and park in the space closest to the front door of the administration building. The bold typeface on the door identified this as a staff car from the Atlanta newspapers. Nelson was back.

"Holy shit," I whispered.

I watched as a short, stocky man with a crew cut, jutting chin, and an assertive manner stepped out of the car and eyed the administration building. He opened the back door of his car, pulled out his suit jacket, and shrugged it over his shoulders. He reached into the front seat and picked up what appeared to be a narrow notebook and slid it into an outside pocket of his suit. He shut the car door and walked up the steps, striding along as if he owned the building.

I turned, saw Wilbur, walked over to him, and said, "The Atlanta newspapers are back. That reporter just went in the front door."

Wilbur's eyes widened. He pushed himself up from the table and said, "I got to go tell the doctors." He waddled down the hall.

A moment later, Wilbur returned, pointed at me, and said, "Do not let him in the receiving ward. If he comes to the door, wave him away. Do not open that door."

"What do I tell him?"

"Tell him we have violent patients on this ward, and we can't be responsible for his safety."

A moment later, Wilbur shouted down the hall, "Coram, come here."

"Dr. Blake wants you in his office," he said. His tone told me he was annoyed. Whatever it was the doctor wanted, Wilbur felt he should deliver, not the college boy. I walked into Dr. Blake's office and saw him pulling box after box of pills from his desk and stacking them on the floor. He was not the patrician, calm, serene man I knew. His voice had gone up a notch, his movements were quick and jerky, and he kept looking at the door as if he were afraid Nelson would crash through any minute. He motioned toward a cabinet and said, "Everything on the top two shelves. Take it out and stack it here."

I opened the cabinet and saw the top shelves were filled with boxes of medicine. "Move fast," Dr. Blake said. When all the boxes were stacked on the floor, Dr. Blake pointed to the stack and said, "Get rid of these. Every box. Do it now."

I had never disposed of a wheelbarrow full of drugs before and did not know if he wanted me to dump the pills in the nearby Oconee

River, scatter them on the back lawn, or ship them to Alabama. I realized I was aiding the doctor in covering his tracks. I realized that what I was doing would make front page news for Jack Nelson. At a remote place I could not articulate, I wished that I were Jack Nelson and could write about an attendant disposing of unapproved drugs. But I never paused, never questioned the doctor's orders. I asked how he wanted me to get rid of the meds.

"Flush them down the toilet. Use the toilet in the patients' bathroom. It is a heavy-duty toilet."

He was right about that. When that thing flushed, it sounded as if someone had pulled a plug at the bottom of the world.

"I have to get a cart."

"Okay, but cover those boxes before you take them to the bathroom. If any patients are in there, chase them out. And have another attendant stand at the door and not let any patients inside."

"Yes, sir."

He told me to flush every pill, to crush the boxes, and put them in a pillowcase, a bag, anything, and to get in my car and go to the city dump and throw the boxes as far as I could.

"Yes, sir."

A half hour later, I came out of the bathroom carrying a bulging pillowcase. Wilbur fell into step beside me. "I know what you are doing," he said. I kept walking and said I was not doing anything.

"Yes, you are. Dr. Blake has been using experimental drugs on patients, and the pharmaceutical houses have been paying him a fortune. Those drugs haven't been approved by the FDA."

I kept walking. I said that Jack Nelson had already written about doctors and experimental drugs and would not do another on the same topic.

Wilbur's voice was urgent when he said, "You don't get it, college boy. It is not the same thing. That story was about experimental drugs on patients in the back wards. It is different from the receiving ward. Doctor Blake is experimenting on people who haven't even been diagnosed. Don't you realize how serious that is?"

I told Wilbur I was following the doctor's orders and that the doctor said I should not talk about what I was doing.

I was walking faster. Wilbur, despite his short legs and great bulk, was matching me step for step. "Hey, college boy, I'm your boss."

"Yes, you are. And Dr. Blake is our boss."

"You ever wonder how many patients he has killed with those illegal drugs? You ever wonder how much money he has made pimping for drug companies?"

"Nope."

"Ever wonder why he has got you doing this?"

I didn't answer. As I unlocked the back door toward the steps, Wilbur got in his parting shot. "That sumbitch is gonna have to get rid of his Mercedes automobile."

In coming days, Nelson wrote more stories about the hospital. But there was no story about the lead physician on the receiving ward who was being paid by pharmaceutical companies to use experimental drugs on new patients. On the receiving ward, we had escaped a visit from Jack Nelson.

A week later, Nelson was back in the hospital. I stood by the window until Nelson returned to his car. As he took off his coat, he turned and looked at the hospital as if storing the memory of that foreboding building in his mind, as if he were trying to see behind locked doors and uncover secrets he knew were there. I wondered if he were looking for me. I wanted to tell him what had happened. I wanted to tell him how much I admired him for coming into this place alone. I was on his side. I wanted to tell him about flushing pills down the toilet in the patients' bathroom. That would be the best part of his story, a story with names and dates and the names of pills not approved by the FDA. Nelson was doing what I wanted to do, and I wanted to help him. But I did not.

More stories came from Nelson, and the tension grew, and the hospital pushed through the greatest turmoil in its history. Every story Nelson wrote reinforced my desire to be a newspaperman. It was time for me to leave the hospital; to finish college and begin my career.

In the receiving ward, life went on as before. I went to the nurses' station every morning, collected and passed out pills to patients. I gave injections. There were fewer shock treatments now, but I assisted with most of them. I still mopped blood and vomit and shit from the floor and walls. Sometimes when doctors wanted a driver, I was chosen. Of course, it was illegal for a doctor to have an attendant acting as his chauffeur. But who was going to tell? I thought it was an honor. And each time a doctor called the head attendant and said he wanted me as a driver, Wilbur came to me and said, "He wanted me to do it. But I told him I have too much to do. I recommended you."

Wilbur was living in his own hell, trapped in the knowledge he had gone as far in this world as he was going to go. He would be an attendant until he grew too old to walk the floor.

All the time I kept thinking of how Jack Nelson had missed the biggest and most sensational part of his story. Jack Nelson was one of the great reporters. He was one of my heroes. He had unearthed the biggest story in Georgia since the Yazoo land fraud. He would later win a Pulitzer Prize for his stories about the hospital. But after the hospital series when I read one of his stories, I wondered what he had missed. I wondered if he had the whole story. I wondered what had been flushed down the toilet.

13

Two dozen student nurses from Georgia Baptist Hospital in Atlanta came to Milledgeville for a psychiatric rotation. The morning after they arrived, Dr. Hood ordered an orientation session and an interview with a patient. I escorted the patient to the large room where this great learning experience would take place.

I had done this before with medical students, and I sat in the back of the room during the sessions. But this business about flushing pills was on my mind, and this day I waited in the hall as the student nurses filed inside. An hour later, they filed from the room. I stood by the door, waiting to retrieve my patient and take him back to the ward.

I saw Mary Catharine Miles the minute she walked out of the door. The thunderbolt hit. She was petite, had short black hair and a look in her eye that said she was trouble. It was the knowing look that comes from being a nursing student and learning the secrets of the human body. It was the look of a young woman with old ideas.

Our eyes met and locked. As she came closer, I got a whiff of her hair. From conversations, I had learned that men often are drawn to a woman because of some specific physical attribute she possesses. Some men like a woman with a large bosom. Some like a woman with long legs, and some men like shapely bottoms. Me? When I

smell a woman's hair, my knees go wobbly, and I hear violins playing. I am captivated by the shampoo-fresh smell of a woman's hair.

Mary Catharine stepped aside so her fellow nurses could pass
and asked, "Is your name Robert?" How did the love of my life,
she of the magic shampoo, know my name?

"Yes."

"Dr. Hood really likes you. He said you were an intellectual."

I was dumbstruck and shook my head in confusion. I had flunked
out of college. How could I be an intellectual? I did not know what
to say. So I mumbled and asked why Dr. Hood was talking about me.

She waited. As her friends passed, some of them looked at Mary
Catharine and smiled. Student nurses, like other wild animals,
know things. After a moment, Mary Catharine said Dr. Hood
was telling the nurses about the hospital and the staff. He said I
was different from the other attendants because I was going back
to college to become a writer.

Mary Catharine and I went out that night and almost every night
afterward. We always wound up in a city park where we found a
dark spot away from the lights. There, we held each other and kissed
long, lingering kisses. We both were aware that she would be here
but a few short months. We never made love. I was always the one
who stopped. It was 1959, and even though I had experienced the
wonderful ways of English girls, I was back home. I was back in
the culture where I grew up, the culture that divided women into
two classes: those who screwed and those who did not.

Perhaps more than anything else, this ancient belief marked me
for what I remained: an unlettered country boy who watched as
the world passed him by.

Our white-hot romance was the talk of the ward, especially
among the nurses. The head nurse smiled at me and said, "When
I see you and Mary Catharine together, I remember what it was
like to be in love."

I stared at her, bewildered, and said, "I thought you were married." She laughed and said she had been married for more than twenty years but that she didn't love her husband twenty-four hours a day; maybe an hour a day.

There was much I had to learn about this love business.

MARY Catherine was the first girl I ever took home to meet my mother. When I called Mother and told her I had met someone and wanted to bring her home, Mother knew I was serious about this girl. Maybe I was ready to settle down. Maybe I was getting straightened out.

Mother said, "Of course, son, bring her home. We are anxious to meet her. And don't worry about Frank. I'll talk to him."

Mary Catharine was from Quincy, Florida, and enjoyed waterskiing. She was horrified when I took her to a scum-covered fish pond—which we called a lake—and told her to make sure she didn't fall when the boat towed her near the swampy area at the far end of the pond. Big alligators lived in there.

Hell, I learned to waterski on this pond. It was the only place I had ever waterskied. But Mary Catharine had learned to waterski on clear lakes in the Florida Panhandle and in the Gulf of Mexico. This pond was a nightmare.

After one pass around the pond, Mary Catharine waved for the boat driver to take her ashore. She coasted to a perfect stop on dry land, stepped out of her skis, and said. "I need a shower."

As we drove back to Milledgeville, Mary Catharine invited me to her hometown to meet her mother. But she wanted to wait until her rotation at Milledgeville ended, and she would have a few days off. We could spend a long weekend at her house. One day we would spend at the beach.

Mary Catharine and I went out almost every night, but always on Friday and Saturday nights. One Friday morning, she called and said she had to cancel our date for that night and for Saturday. Sunday afternoon, she called, and we went for a walk, and she told me she had a boyfriend from Atlanta who had driven down for the weekend. They spent most of their time in a motel. Guess I called that one wrong when I thought she didn't screw.

"Will you still go home with me?" she asked. "I've never taken a boy home, and I want you to meet my mother."

I said, "Yes." But I wondered why she wanted to take me home when she had never taken her boyfriend from Atlanta home. Maybe he was just someone to take her out on weekends and take her to bed. I tried to be blasé about this. But I was confused. I think she was too.

ONE of the patients on the receiving ward was about forty, slender, with glistening dark hair that always remained in place. He had a smile like a movie star. He was the smoothest and slickest-talking person I'd ever met, so convincing that if he'd told me the sun would rise in the west tomorrow, I would have gotten up the next morning and looked to the west.

His name was William. But when he met someone, he smiled that dazzling smile, stuck out his hand, and said, "Please call me Billy." If he was talking to a man, he clasped that man's elbow as he talked, stared at the man as if he were the most important person in the world, and he and the man were instant friends.

Billy was meticulous about his personal appearance. His khakis always pressed. His smile always glued on. His personality always in dazzle mode. But his eyes never smiled. He was diagnosed as having a psychopathic personality, and like most psychopaths, he was always trying to game the system. The more I learned about psychopaths, the scarier they became. Not because of possible physical violence, but because they left mayhem and confusion in their wake and they never looked back. They never felt remorse.

They never felt contrition. They never accepted responsibility. They had no conscience. They didn't care.

I looked at Billy's record and saw that his brother had sworn out a lunacy warrant against him and had him committed. Talking about his brother disturbed Billy. We attendants stopped conversations when a patient became upset. But Billy was classified as nonviolent. He had no heart and no soul. But he was not violent.

Billy was horrified that he might receive shock treatment. He was Mr. Nice Guy every moment. But he knew that soon he would be transferred to one of the back wards, and he knew that once he was behind those locked doors, he would never see the outside world again.

Billy also knew I was bat shit over Mary Catharine and that I was embarrassed about driving her to Florida in my old smoke-belching Mercury. The trip was more than two hundred miles, and the costs in gas and oil would be considerable.

One morning, Billy pulled me aside, flashed his pearly smile, and with some deference said, "When you take Mary Catharine home to Quincy, how would you like to take her in a nice car?"

I looked at him in bewilderment.

"I can get you one," he said. "I will lend it to you."

I snorted and reminded Billy that he was a patient and there was no way he could get me a car. The idea was ludicrous.

Billy looked around to make sure no one could overhear us. He leaned closer and in a confidential whisper said, "Sign me out of here one morning. You can do that. Let's go to Atlanta in your car; then I'll follow you back in my car. It's a Cadillac. I will park it here so you can use it. It will be fine. I plan to be out of here soon and want my car to be ready."

"I can't sign you out."

Billy smiled and said I signed out patients every day. I could sign him out. That was different; I was taking them to another ward or to the medical floor. Not to Atlanta.

"Who will know besides us?"

When I did not answer, he pressed his advantage. "Look, it's maybe a two-hour drive to Atlanta. We leave one morning right after breakfast. We won't be in Atlanta more than an hour. Back here midafternoon, and no one ever knows we were gone. It's good for both of us. You can drive my car to Quincy. And the car will be here when I am released."

Numerous problems surrounded his idea, one being attendants were not allowed to take patients on joyrides. And I knew Billy was not going to be released. Not in my lifetime. On the more immediate practical side: where would a patient park his car at a mental institution?

Psychopaths have a unique ability to sniff out the gullible. That is why Billy zeroed in on me. I had a weak will, was naive, and wanted to impress Mary Catharine's mother. I was tired of failures in my life and wanted once, just once, to do something that other people appreciated. A new car might do that. The car might also impress Mary Catharine. I gave in as Billy knew I would. On Wednesday morning, two days before I was going to Florida with Mary Catharine, I told Billy I liked his plan. We would go to Atlanta tomorrow.

The minute I agreed, I knew I was in trouble. Just as I had known I was in trouble when I took a load of furniture off base to sell in Liverpool. But dark winds were pushing me, and I rushed toward my punishment.

I signed him out, put him in my car, and we were off. As we chatted, he remained as deferential as he had been on the ward. Two hours later, we entered Avondale Estates, a suburb in east Atlanta. Billy pointed toward a used car lot and said, "Pull in there."

"Why?"

"So I can pick up my car."

"Stay here," he said as he stepped out of the car and walked up to a salesman. The dynamics of my relationship with Billy had shifted, and a frisson of anxiety chilled me.

Billy and the salesman grinned at each other for a few minutes, chatting easily. The salesman pointed toward a row of cars, and he and Billy walked along, the salesman discussing the merits of each. I stepped out of the car so I could better see them. The salesman waved. Billy looked at me and did not smile.

We had not been there ten minutes when Billy picked out a Cadillac, a big two-toned land yacht, said he wanted it, then slapped at his pocket in an annoyed way. "I forgot my checkbook," he said. "Would you let me write a counter check?"

I did not know what a counter check was. But the salesman never paused. "Which bank?" he asked. Billy named the biggest bank in Atlanta.

"Sure, just write your account number in the upper left-hand corner."

"Of course." Billy acted as if he did this every day. I could not help but admire how smooth and slick he was. I watched in astonishment as he filled out the check and gave it to the salesman. The salesman studied the check for maybe ten seconds, handed Billy the title and the keys. The two men shook hands. Billy fired up the Cadillac and eased down the driveway. As he passed me, I rolled down the window to tell him we had to return to Milledgeville. But he was quicker. "Follow me," he said. "I have a quick errand."

I was reeling. Billy had just written a bad check for thousands of dollars and driven off in a late-model Cadillac. I wanted to jump out of the car and shout to the salesman, "This guy is a patient at Milledgeville. He has no bank account and no money. He is a whack job." But I was more concerned with regaining control of my patient.

I followed Billy through Avondale, on to Ponce de Leon, and then right on Briarcliff. Where the hell was he going?

About two miles later, he turned left onto a quiet residential street. Small white houses lined both sides. Billy rolled into the driveway of a well-kept house. As he stepped out, he waved at me and said, "You stay there. I won't be a minute. Soon as I get back, we will go to Milledgeville."

He did not knock. He pushed open the door and entered. About ten seconds later, I heard fierce shouting and thumps and bumps that sounded as if furniture were being moved about.

Billy stood in the door, his shirt ripped from his body. He was breathing hard. As he ran to his car, he waved for me to back up. "I whipped my brother's ass. He's calling the cops. We have to go."

The first thing that came to my mind was that, contrary to what I had been told, psychopaths can be violent. I recovered quickly and said, "Okay, drive down to Ponce, turn left, and follow me to Milledgeville." The small matter of the police coming after Billy was a bit of a concern.

He nodded. "Lead the way."

And I did. That is, until we got to where Ponce split and Scott Boulevard went to the left. I went right and saw Billy turn left. I looked over my shoulder as he accelerated, and my first thought was, "He must know a short cut."

My second thought was "That son of a bitch has eloped."

14

THE trip from Atlanta back to Milledgeville was the longest two hours of my life. There was no good ending to what was about to happen. Once again, I had gone stupid. At the hospital, I parked in the rear of the staff parking lot and hoped no one from the receiving ward would recognize my car. I slumped in my seat and locked my eyes on the entrance, hoping Billy would return but knowing he would not. There I sat for a half day.

As the late afternoon turned to dusk and then to darkness, I hung my head and faced the truth: Billy had eloped. I had signed him out of the hospital, and he had gone rabbit. How could anyone my age be so naive?

By now, Wilbur had done a head count and knew Billy was missing. He knew I had signed Billy out and that I was nowhere to be seen. I trudged up the walkway, up the elevator, and unlocked the door to the receiving ward. Wilbur was at the far end of the hall and saw me open the door. His little pig eyes never left my face as I walked down that long hall. I told Wilbur straight out that I had taken Billy to Atlanta and that Billy had eloped.

He shook his head in disbelief. He was appalled and delighted. "I think you better go to your room and stay there. Tomorrow the administration will decide what we are going to do with you." He started to walk away, then turned back to me. "Be in Dr. Blake's office at nine o'clock tomorrow morning." He paused and sounded pleased when he said, "It's always you college boys who fuck up."

What did he know about college boys? He had been on the ward for twenty years. But he did have a point. He also had a job. I was about to lose mine.

I decided at that moment to go ahead with my plans to take Mary Catharine to Quincy over the weekend. Being with the most exciting woman in the world was more important than hanging around here waiting for the hammer of doom.

I packed a small bag, called Mary Catharine, and told her what I had done.

"Oh, Robert. You had so much." Her words bored into my heart. I had the best job in the air force until I screwed up. I had a good job here until today. I squeezed my eyes shut, determined to make this weekend work. I shook my head to clear away the guilt and the anger and asked her to meet me at her front door tomorrow morning as soon after 8:00 a.m. as possible. We had a long drive to Quincy. Monday, I would drive her to the hospital in Atlanta, find a boarding house for me, look for a job, and return to college.

I packed my clothes, slipped out the door, and put the bag in my car. I did not want anyone seeing me with a bag tomorrow morning. At a pay phone, I called Mother and asked if I could borrow her car for the weekend. I would leave my car at her house, drive her new car to Quincy, and return it Monday.

Mother now had a new baby, a little girl. Mary Catharine and I had to look at the baby and tell Mother and Frank how beautiful she was. Frank could have listened to those compliments all day. Mary Catharine hugged Frank, and he was bouncing from one foot to the other, his deeply wrinkled face trying to smile. Mother kept looking from Mary Catharine to me, and when I gave her a goodbye hug, she whispered, "Son, I think she is the one." I smiled, and then Mary Catharine and I were off for Quincy, crossing deep southwest Georgia into the Florida Panhandle.

Mary Catharine had an endearing habit when we were driving. She sat so close to me that our legs and shoulders touched. Occasionally, she leaned over and kissed me on the neck.

"Tonight, after Mother goes to sleep, I am coming to your room," she whispered.

All I could muster was, "Okay."

As we came into Quincy, I saw a police car parked perpendicular to the road, the officer watching traffic entering town.

Mary Catharine told me I was the first man she had ever brought home and that her mother, whose husband had walked out on her when Mary Catharine was a baby, would ask me a lot of questions. She did not want her daughter to repeat her mistake in picking the wrong man.

Mary Catharine and her mother lived in a small and neat house on the south side of town. After the pleasantries were exchanged and I was shown my room, Mary Catharine's mother said she had planned a picnic on the beach for the three of us. We were discussing details of the trip when the phone rang. Mary Catharine's mother answered, went rigid, said, "Just a moment," and handed the phone to me. "Your mother," she said. The phone was in the living room, so Mary Catharine and her mother heard every word I said.

"Mother?"

"Robert, what did you do?" Mother wailed. "The sheriff called me and said the police in Milledgeville called him trying to find you. They know where you are, and the police in Quincy are looking for your car. I told them to hold off, and I would make sure you got back up to Milledgeville. What did you do?" She was on the edge of tears. "Frank is so mad with you."

I cupped my hand around the phone and whispered, "I'll be back Sunday afternoon."

"No, I told the sheriff you would be back now. He knows us and vouched for you with the sheriff up in Milledgeville. But if I don't tell them you are on the way back right now, they are going to Mary Catharine's house and arrest you." She sobbed. "The police down there are looking for your car. I did not tell them you were in my car."

I couldn't explain this with Mary Catharine's mother a few feet away. "I'll leave right now," I said. "When I get to Edison, I will tell you all about it."

"What did you do?" she wailed.

"I let a patient escape," I whispered.

"Escape?" Mother cried. "You mean a patient from the crazy house got away from you? You mean a crazy person is out there in public?"

One of the most difficult conversations of my life was telling Mary Catharine's mother that I had to return to Milledgeville. I had not been in the house a half hour. I could give her no reason for my leaving except to say, "Something has come up that I have to see about."

Mary Catharine asked, "Is it about Billy?"

I nodded. Mary Catharine looked at her mother and said, "I'll tell you about it."

"How will you get to Atlanta?" I asked.

"Ride the bus to Atlanta and then find someone to drive me to Milledgeville to pick up my things." That someone would be her boyfriend in Atlanta. She was subdued, and I sensed that our relationship had hit a big rock. I was the first man she ever brought home and couldn't stay because the police were looking for me.

The drive to Edison was long and painful. Almost as painful as the conversation with Mother and Frank. He was upset because Mother was upset and she should not be upset with a new baby. He gave me a hard look, the same look accountants give prospective car buyers who don't have good credit, and said, "Robert, when is this going to end?"

I wondered the same thing. I was a twenty-one-year-old problem child. Flunked out of college. Kicked out of the air force, and now the police were looking for me.

"They want you to call them at the hospital and tell them what time you will be back," Mother said.

A deputy sheriff was waiting in the hospital parking lot when I arrived. He charged me with facilitating the escape of a patient. It was a misdemeanor charge, and my trial date was three weeks away. "The sheriff in your county said he knows your family and that you will show up for the trial."

I nodded. "I will be there."

"You better. If you are not, the judge will issue a bench warrant, and we will come looking for you."

The deputy escorted me back to the ward where Wilbur took some delight in informing me, "You are terminated. Effective immediately."

Hell, I knew that one was coming. I also knew that I had caused great embarrassment to the hospital, the doctors on the floor, and to the nurses. They had encouraged me about going back to college and talked with me in ways they'd never talked with the other attendants.

I slept in my car that night. Early the next morning, I took my car to the dealer, told him I had no job and no way of making payments, so I was turning in the car. I handed him the keys.

He looked at the keys, looked at me, and said, "People don't usually turn in a car. They just stop paying, and we have to go get the car."

The twelve-hour bus ride back to Edison seemed to last a week. Edison did not have a bus station. The bus stopped at a downtown service station, where I got off. I walked the two miles to the house.

The fear and apprehension of the upcoming trial hung over the house like a biblical plague. Countless times, Mother—her baby in her arms—asked, "Robert, what do you think they will do?"

And countless times, I said, "I don't know." I was more concerned about not seeing Mary Catharine again. She was back in class and difficult to reach on the telephone. And she had a distant tone in her voice when we talked. But once this legal thing was solved, I would move to Atlanta, and we would see each other again.

Frank, the typical mild-mannered and soft-spoken bookkeeper, wanted to throw me out. He glared at me, muttering under his breath, and at night behind the bedroom door, I heard him saying to Mother, "But he's twenty-one. He should be out on his own."

"Don't raise your voice. You are upsetting the baby." Mother paused and said in a voice that left no room for argument, "Frank, he is my son. We have to see him through this. Then we can talk about it."

"What does he want to do with his life? What job does he want?" Frank's voice was plaintive. Mother paused a moment, knowing what Frank's reaction would be. She said I had mentioned to her that I wanted to work for a newspaper.

That was the dumbest thing Frank had ever heard. His dismissive snort was what Mother expected.

The day of my trial arrived. Because of the baby, Mother could not go. She told Frank to drive me to Milledgeville and sit with me through the hearing. "And take some money," she ordered. "If he doesn't go to jail, he will have to pay a fine."

On that long trip, the only words between Frank and me were when we drove into Milledgeville and I gave him instructions on how to reach the courthouse.

Frank stood beside me when my case was called, and I stared up the judge. It took fewer than five minutes for the judge to fine me $100 and put me on probation for a year. Given that I had released a patient from a mental institution, it was a light sentence. But the hospital wanted this to go away in a quick and quiet manner. The hospital had been in the newspapers enough for the past few months and did not want the public to know that attendants were releasing psychopaths into the general population. They wanted this over and done with and the miscreant attendant sent out of town.

Frank flinched when he heard the amount of the fine, and his face was pinched as he reached into his wallet and handed the money to a bailiff.

It is a measure of my insensitivity that while I was glad Frank had paid my fine, I was more concerned about what this would do for Mary Catharine and me. She had a boyfriend in Atlanta. She had no future with a man fired from the lowly job of attendant at a mental hospital—a man with no job, no degree, and no prospects. Somehow, I had missed that part of life when I could be described as a promising young man.

On the long ride back to Edison, I stretched out in the back seat and wept. I wept because I had flunked out of college. I wept because I had served three sentences in a military stockade. I wept because I had been kicked out of the air force. I wept because I had been fired from Milledgeville. I wept because I knew I had lost Mary Catharine. I wept because I had never grown up. I wept because I had no future.

Every time I looked up, Frank's knuckles were squeezing the steering wheel. He ground his false teeth and muttered. But he said not a word to me. When he drove into the driveway at the house and turned off the ignition, he paused for a moment, then twisted in the seat, looked at me, and said, "I want you gone."

Two days later, I was packed and ready to catch the once-a-week Trailways bus that would take me to Albany and then, after a half-dozen stops, to Atlanta. Mother knew I had no money. As I walked out the door, she handed me $300. "That is the last money you will ever get from me," she said. "Don't call and don't ask me for more. You are on your own."

She reached out, clasped my arm, looked me square in the eye, and said, "And, son, I don't want you to come home again until you are straightened out."

"You don't want me to come home anymore?"

She shook her head and raised her voice so Frank could hear. And I knew that what she said was coming from Frank. I couldn't blame him. He did not sign up for this. If our situations had been reversed, I would have done what he was doing. All Frank wanted was an unruffled existence. He wanted to get up every morning, have his breakfast, go tend the books at the Chevrolet place, and come home to dinner and maybe a few cooing noises with his infant daughter. He wanted to have a drink of the bourbon he hid in a shaving lotion jar. What Mother said came from Frank, but it broke her heart.

I stood in the doorway. "Mother." My voice was anguished. "Are you disowning me?"

In southwest Georgia, a mother did not banish her children. This was biblical shit. Mother's eyes filled with tears. But she was strong and could do what she had to do.

"Robert, you are my son. My oldest child. And I will always love you. But I don't want you in this house until you are straightened out."

She wavered, closed her eyes, put out a hand against the door for support. "I have to lie down," she said.

"Do I . . .?" Frank said, concern on his face.

Mother waved him away and turned toward the bedroom. "I'm all right. Take Robert to the bus station and come on back home."

Frank glared at me. "Let's go."

As I threw my suitcase into the back seat, I wondered again what *straightened out* meant. I had heard that from the sarge and heard it from Mother and still was not sure what it meant. I climbed in the back seat. I did not want to sit up front with Frank. That was fine with him. As we drove into Edison, I kept wondering about this straightened out stuff. I had heard that from the sarge until the day he died. Now Mother was saying the same thing. And Frank agreed.

We had a consensus.

15

I was bound for Atlanta to get a job, return to college, and at last begin the process of becoming a newspaper reporter.

I had left home before, to college and to the air force, and then to Milledgeville. But each time, I knew I would be returning to my hometown. Now my mother had disowned me and cut whatever psychic bonds I had with Edison, a town that forever afterward would be an alien place to me. Atlanta would become my new home.

As with many young men of the time who moved to Atlanta, the only place I could afford was a boarding house, a place where I would have a room and where breakfast and dinner would be provided. The tiny, white-haired widow who ran the boarding house—and all boarding houses then were run by widows—was apologetic when she showed me the only available room. The plump little lady wrung her hands and said the room was so small that she was uncomfortable charging me the regular boarding fee. But she was not uncomfortable enough to lower the fee. She smiled and said the other tenants were like me, young men getting started in life.

My room was the size of a large closet. A single bed. A small chest of drawers. And a wheeled device with a rod across the top where I hung my clothes. The bathroom was down the hall and shared with two other tenants.

Sharing a bathroom is up near the top of the list of things I did not want to do. But I had no choice.

Finding a job and entering college was easy. I did not care what the job was, as long as it could finance my way through college. Within two days, I was working at a trucking company coding cargo for delivery routes.

I bought a subscription to the *Atlanta Constitution*, and every morning at breakfast, I read the paper from front to back, unconsciously emulating my dad. The big difference was that my dad had considered McGill's column to be irrational nonsense. I considered it scripture. And my dad thought the paper to be "bum fodder." I thought it was a lighthouse whose beam pierced the darkness.

I enrolled in night school at Georgia State College in downtown Atlanta, a school with an enrollment of fewer than five thousand students, more than half of whom worked full-time jobs and attended night school. After a day's work, I was too tired to carry a full load of classes. I took two classes. Most of the classrooms were in an old parking garage, and I walked up or down a circular ramp to attend classes.

My boarding house was two miles from Georgia Baptist Hospital where Mary Catharine was in training. But it might as well have been a hundred miles.

I did not have a car, and for a date, I had to borrow the car of a fellow at the boarding house. But I could borrow it during the week as he used it on weekends. After several dates, Mary Catharine gently told me she was serious about her Atlanta boyfriend. She did not add the obvious: her boyfriend had a car and a job. I was the almost-fling she had at Milledgeville, the guy who was a placeholder until she returned to Atlanta, the loser guy fired from the lowest and most menial job at a mental hospital.

She told me not to call her again. But I did. When the nurses on her floor heard my voice ask for Mary Catharine, they hung up. And then they began to tell me Mary Catharine was out with her boyfriend.

But I continued to call. And when I discovered Mary Catharine was about to graduate, I sent her an expensive scarab bracelet—then the height of jewelry fashion—that I could not afford. I went to the graduation ceremony in a nearby church. The graduates and their families sat on the main level in the auditorium. No one but me was sitting in the balcony. My eyes were locked on Mary Catharine who, after one glance, would not look at me again. Some of the other nurses knew who I was and nudged each other and pointed and smiled in pity.

I was late in accepting the fact she had dumped me. And when I did, I wailed and moaned and moped and wept as if it were the end of the world. You might think I was so experienced at being dumped that it did not bother me. But it did. I was mortally wounded. I immersed myself in my studies.

The next two years were a series of menial jobs and menial boarding houses, of eating breakfast every morning and dinner every night with young men on the way up and with a few middle-aged men on the way down. The family-style meals were served by widows bitter about being relegated to a back bedroom while boarders filled every available space in their homes, bitter that their husbands had left them no money. Their blood was turning to vinegar as they toddled toward the grave.

One Friday afternoon, a friend from Edison called. He was finishing college at Emory and said he was going home for the weekend. Did I want to ride with him? I had not been to Edison in several years and on a whim decided to go. No suitcase, not even a toothbrush. My idea was to use Edison to help me establish more bona fides for Atlanta. And I could best do that by having a good credit rating. I had my friend drop me off at the bank—I never went home—and inside I walked to the desk of the president. I had known him since childhood. I told him I wanted to borrow $100 and that I would pay him back twenty dollars a month. He nodded and mused and pulled at his ear and looked at the ceiling and then launched a ten-minute lecture about the responsibility inherent in borrowing money. I was borrowing $100, and I wondered what sort of lecture accompanied a loan for $1,000. At the end of the lecture, I signed the papers, and he gave me $100.

I walked to the edge of town and hitchhiked with a farmer who was going to Columbus. It was dusk when he dropped me off near the airport where I was seized by the idea of chartering an airplane to Atlanta. I had never flown in a small aircraft before, and this seemed a good opportunity. The charter fee was $80. The flight was worth it. Flying in a black night over rural southwest Georgia was the aerial version of my early life: I wanted to get away from the darkness. Then from a distance, I saw the lights of Atlanta appearing, a broad and bright splash against the darkness. An airport is easy to find at night: from a distance, it is a black hole surrounded by bright lights. Voices came through the speakers, magnified and warped by the radio until they were unintelligible. But the pilot understood. We lined up for the active runway and descended into the busy Atlanta airport. It was an experience I would never forget. I vowed that someday I would learn to fly an airplane.

At the airport, I caught a taxi to my boarding house. The taxi cost ten dollars. I arrived with ten dollars remaining from my loan. The financial responsibility thing did not resonate with me.

I changed boarding houses every three months or so because I was restless, unanchored, and anxious. I was fired from three jobs during the first several years in Atlanta—every job I had during that time. I don't remember all the jobs, and I don't remember why I was fired, but I think it was because I looked upon my bosses as later models of my dad: men of authority, men who wanted things done their way, men who often were remote from entry-level employees.

I rode the bus every morning and continued to read the *Constitution*. In the afternoon or after my second class at Georgia State, I read the *Journal* on the bus back to the boarding house. And I hoped and dreamed that one day I might get a job with one of the Atlanta papers.

The hope was dim, and the dream seemed impossible.

By the time I finished my sophomore year, I had a respectable job training to be an underwriter at a downtown insurance company. I lived on the second floor of a respectable boarding house on Fourteenth Street, and I had saved enough money for a down payment on a respectable car, a Sprite, a little shoebox of a sports car from the Austin-Healy family. But best of all, I was writing a weekly column in the *Signal*, the Georgia State newspaper. A friend was editor and needed a columnist. He said, "Hey, aren't you studying journalism? Don't you want to work for a newspaper? Here's your chance."

This was the first time I had written anything on a regular basis, and I put much thought and time into the column. I wrote a column about the need for political leaders to pull Georgia away from her prejudices and mistreatment of minorities. Another about holding onto one's convictions while being pressured from every direction. Another about the need for greater moral strength in students.

I received an award from the journalism department for writing the best column of the year. The column was about an appearance of a Scottish bagpipe band in the city auditorium. When I asked the dean of students for permission and money to start a literary magazine, he agreed. Thus was born the *Credo*, a yearly publication that remains but today is of far better quality than it was that first year.

At my boarding house on Fourteenth Street, both men and women were tenants. In the basement apartment was a Georgia

Tech student working on his PhD. On the second floor, my floor, was a recent graduate of Florida State University who worked for the Atlanta office of Macmillan publishing company, a prestigious job, as Macmillan had published *Gone with the Wind*, a book of great significance in Atlanta.

Her name was Leslie Lowell. Her room was the first on the left after going through the sitting room and down a long hall. A bathroom was the second room. Mine was the third room. There was no tenant in the fourth room. Leslie and I shared a bathroom and a kitchen.

Given that Leslie and I had to knock on the bathroom door before we entered, we soon became friends. She never asked me to put the toilet seat down, and I never asked her to leave it up. It was at breakfast that we deepened our friendship. One morning, I was eating a bowl of oatmeal and reading the paper when she walked in. She wore a skirt and jacket, heels, and the look of a career woman. She had short, well-kept hair, a direct gaze, and a prominent chin that revealed her strength of purpose and her character.

After an exchange of pleasantries, and after she prepared a quick breakfast, she sat across from me at the table. I folded my newspaper and put it aside. "You don't have to do that for me," she said. "In the morning, I am not much for conversation."

But she was. We chatted about her job, my job, my going to night school and wanting to work at a newspaper, and a dozen other things. But what I most remember was the small gold key she wore around her neck. I asked her what it was.

She fingered the key. "My Phi Beta Kappa key." She shrugged almost in apology. "I was inducted my last year at college."

My eyes widened. I am sure that every young man has something he admires. I admired intelligence. And Leslie was the first Phi Beta Kappa I had ever met. To be a member of that scholastic society meant she was smart. I had no standing to be a snob about anything. But I liked smarts, and I was a snob about people who were not smart.

I wanted to ask Leslie out. But she was engaged to a man she had met at Florida State. He lived in Florida, but they wrote each other and often talked by phone. The phone was on the wall across from my room, and I could not help but overhear their conversations.

She and her fiancé were on the way up. I had just gotten off probation and was keeping a low profile. Leslie and I were the same age, but I was a sophomore in college and working at a menial job in an insurance company.

If I wanted to date her, it could not be a regular date. It had to be something with no hint of romance, just an outing with the person who shared her bathroom.

We agreed to climb Stone Mountain one morning and watch the sunrise. Why she went out with me, I do not know. I read the morning paper. She read the *American Scholar.* I ripped around town and smoked and drank. She was a Christian Scientist.

What we had in common you could poke up a gnat's ass and still have room for two caraway seeds and a Volkswagen. But nothing propinks like propinquity. A few months later, she broke her engagement, and we made wedding plans. Frank and Mother came up for the wedding, but Frank sat outside in the car and would not come into the church. Leslie started her period on the way to the wedding, and she spent our wedding night pacing the floor, bent over with the pain of menstrual cramps.

16

Leslie grew weary of my talking about how one day I would be a writer. "You can be a writer now," she said. "If you are going to write, then write."

I said nobody would take my work, that the only place I had been published was in the college newspaper and a poem in the literary magazine.

"Take the initiative," she said. "Go down to *Atlanta Magazine* and write an article for them."

I looked at her as if she had lost her mind. *Atlanta Magazine* was the hottest city magazine in the country. The legendary editor Jim Townsend was bringing in the best writers in the South, and they considered it a privilege to write for the magazine. For Atlantans, the magazine was mandatory reading. Why would the magazine accept a piece from a college student who had never published?

"You won't know unless you try," she said.

I called the magazine and told the receptionist I wanted to talk to the editor about a story. She said, "What story is that?"

When I said, "I don't know. He hasn't told me what he wants me to write," she struggled not to giggle.

"You should write a story first and then submit it," she said. As if talking to a not-very-bright child, she said, "We call that writing a piece on speculation. If we like it, we will buy it."

"Oh." Pause. "Okay."

A few days later, I was having a hot dog at the Varsity, a hamburger, hot dog, milkshake, and fried-pie joint that was popular in Atlanta. It was often filled with students from nearby Georgia

Tech. I looked around at the choreographed movements of the kitchen staff, the waiters, and heard the carhops who had their own vernacular when they shouted in orders. "Walk me a dog" was a hot dog to go. "A naked steak" was a bare hamburger.

An older man dressed in a suit sat in a small, glass-enclosed office. He appeared engrossed in paperwork. But occasionally he jumped from his desk and went out on the floor and talked to a cook or a server. He had some sort of internal radar about operations, and I figured he was the manager. Turned out he was the owner. His name was Frank Gordy. And he was amenable to my writing a story about his business.

"No one has ever written about us," he said. "I don't know why."

I told him I was doing a piece for *Atlanta Magazine*. I didn't tell him I had never been published there and was writing this story on speculation. His eyes lit up, and he gave me a behind-the-counter tour of the restaurant, told me how many hot dogs a day he served, and that his special-order ice cream had the highest butterfat content of any ice cream in Atlanta. Frank Gordy's children worked there and one day would take over the business. He talked of the Georgia Tech students he had fed for free because he knew that when they graduated, they would bring their families back, and he would have another generation of customers.

I spent several weeks writing the piece and then mailed it to the magazine. A few days later, the managing editor called and said the magazine was putting together a special issue on Georgia Tech and that in all their planning sessions, no one had thought of a piece on the Varsity. It was a natural. "We want to publish the piece," he said. "We will pay you fifty dollars. We pay on publication, so it will be several months."

Leslie was the impetus behind my first sale as a writer.

My journalism professor was a small, frail woman whose day job was working on the copy desk at the *Journal*. I wish I could remember her name. That I don't bears witness to the fact that "rim rats"—those who sit around the curved copy desk—are faceless and nameless. She had a preoccupied air about her and was a fanatic about spelling, in particular, names and proper nouns. To misspell someone's name was unforgivable. "Ask," she said. "Nobody objects to spelling their own name."

Infractions in grammar made her weep. She taught clarity above all else. She taught the inverted-pyramid style of writing a news story: make sure the lede comes first. Don't bury it. Make sure the facts in the story are in descending order of importance. "That way, if we have to cut a story to fit into the paper, we can slice from the bottom without affecting the piece."

She must have had a sinus disorder because she wiped her nose every few minutes. She came to class one night carrying the latest edition of the *Signal*, put her books on her desk, wiped her nose, held up the paper, and said, "Robert, I liked your column in this issue."

"Thank you," I said, embarrassed. I had rarely been complimented for anything. But to be complimented for my writing, and by someone who worked at the *Journal*, well, I glowed as if I had been scrubbed with uranium.

She wiped her nose again and, still looking down at her desk, said, "In fact, I like most of your columns."

After she complimented me in front of the class, my fellow journalism students snickered and derided me as a teacher's pet. And I learned that one's fellow writers—or in this case, fellow journalism students—are jealous sons of bitches who will love you for your mediocrity but resent you for your talent.

Some students in the class were dabbling, taking what they thought was an easy course. They did not have the calling and would never work in journalism. Some students thought they wanted to be writers, but in reality, they were having a hot flash and would move on to major in business or English. Some students were true believers and prayed that after they graduated, they would maybe find a job a job at a small weekly paper and then, if the gods smiled upon them, get an interview maybe with a paper in Macon or Savannah or Columbus. The Atlanta papers were in a firmament beyond a student's dreams.

ONE night, my journalism professor asked me to stay after class. Being asked to stay after class is the academic version of a mercy killing. It means the student is either in academic trouble or that he shows such an abysmal lack of reporting skills or writing ability that he should consider another major.

I watched the professor during class. She sniffed often, and the sniff was always followed by wiping her nose with a Kleenex. After the Kleenex reached what she considered the maximum saturation point, she stuffed it into the bulging pocket of her jacket.

I sat at my desk until the last student left the classroom. The professor raised her head, smiled, and waved for me to come to her desk. She was collecting her books and papers and shoveling them into her briefcase. She did not look up when she said, "Robert, we have an opening for a new reporter at the *Journal*. Would you be interested?"

I sucked in my breath. I froze and stared at the floor.

In my heart, I had wondered if my dream of becoming a reporter for one of the Atlanta newspapers was a bridge too far. I wondered if I had what it took to be a reporter for a major metropolitan daily. The aura of the papers was such that I believed only the most talented and most aggressive and the best writers would be offered a job at this tabernacle of journalism. I was a raggedy-assed, shirttail young man from southwest Georgia. I was not good enough to work in the same building as Ralph McGill.

And now, as a college sophomore, I was asked if I wanted to apply for an opening at the paper. I knew that if I got this job, it would be my career. I would stay forever.

"It's two years before I graduate," I mumbled.

"You can keep going to night school. There may be an occasional conflict if you are covering a breaking story at night. But I think you can do it."

This was too much too fast. An overload of emotion. I managed to mumble, "Yes, ma'am. I would love that chance." I was still staring at the floor.

She touched my arm and smiled in understanding. "You'll do okay, Robert. You are a good writer. I wouldn't have recommended you if you weren't."

She wiped her nose, leaving a streak of slimy moisture across her upper lip. I was from southwest Georgia, and I didn't know much. But I knew she should be using a fresh Kleenex.

THE next time my journalism class met, the professor called me to her desk, leaned toward me, handed me a piece of paper, and whispered, "This is the name of the city editor and the time for your interview with him."

I stared at the scrap of paper. It took me a moment to speak. "Thank you."

She wiped her nose.

When I sat down, the student in the next chair grinned and said, "So you are passing notes with the teacher?"

THE things I can't forget are so much stronger than the things I remember. And I can't forget, will never forget, the headlong rush of emotions during my first visit to the newsroom of the *Atlanta Journal*.

Now I was in a chair in the city room, listening to the sounds of a newspaper on deadline. I was there, head in my hands, remembering my past, hoping Harold Davis would not pry into my background.

I saw a pair of shoes in front of me, looked up, and there was Harold Davis. "I'm sorry to keep you waiting," he said. He pointed to a desk at the back of the city room. "That desk is empty. Let's sit there."

I followed him through the city room. He pulled a chair from an adjacent desk, said, "Have a seat," then sat behind the desk, turned, and faced me. He was soft-spoken but all business. He was a smart guy who had heard every bullshit story in the universe, and his eyes did not blink as he stared at me. I don't remember much about the interview. But I do remember that Davis said he had read my columns and liked them. He said, if I was hired, I would have to sometimes work late into the evening and would that affect my classes.

"No. If I miss any classes, I can make them up," I said.

He looked at me for a long moment, and I had the feeling he could look into a person's eyes and know all he needed to know. The city editor of a major metropolitan daily, any metropolitan daily, is a person with lots of hard bark on him.

He said the *Journal* was an afternoon paper and put out four issues of the paper every day: the early edition, the final home, the state edition, and the street edition, the last of which was called the "blue streak." He said, "We are on deadline from the time we walk in the door until we put out the 'blue streak' late in the afternoon." If a reporter was on a breaking story, he had to call in a new lede for every edition. Dictate it over the phone from his notes. He paused, and his eyes narrowed a bit as he said, "Not everyone can stand up under that sort of pressure." He raised his eyebrows in a question mark.

"I think I can do that."

"Have you written anything other than for the college paper?"

I shrugged. "I have a piece coming out in *Atlanta Magazine* in a couple of months."

He could not hide his surprise. He looked around the newsroom. "I don't think we have anyone on staff who has written for that magazine." He paused. "A lot of them would like to."

When he turned his gaze back on me, his face had a hint of respect.

He stood up and told me to go down to the personnel department and fill out the paperwork, and he would be in touch. He paused. "We will see what you got."

17

I sat at a desk in the personnel department, a stack of forms before me. One by one I turned the pages of the job application, wanting to get an idea about the type of questions asked. Buried deep in the stack was a page with a small box asking about prior military experience. I paused over that section and decided to leave it blank. On another page was a form asking about previous employment. I did not include Milledgeville. Nor did I note that I had been fired and was tried in court and that I had been on probation for a year. And I did not mention the three jobs from which I had been fired in Atlanta. I wrote of my present job with the insurance company.

I hoped that because I was a college student that these empty boxes would go unnoticed. After all, I was too young to have a background.

I lied on my job application. I lied multiple times. They were lies of omission, but they were still lies.

When I handed the forms to the woman in charge, she smiled and said, "We will be in touch."

A week later, the city editor called and said, "How soon can you come to work?" I told him my employer had such a large turnover of college students that they required no notice: I could be at the *Journal* on Monday morning.

In the beginning, I did what every new reporter does: I wrote obits. I rewrote wire copy. I wrote little briefs. And I counted the days until I might have a regular beat or be a general assignment reporter. Soon I was covering civic club meetings and writing three- and four-paragraph filler stories.

From the beginning, I was an aggressive reporter. I knew there was always more to the story. No matter how good a reporter might be, no matter how much he knew about the subject he was writing about, no matter how many people he interviewed, no matter how much research he did, there was always one more question, always one more thing, because, somewhere, someone was flushing pills down the toilet.

On every interview, even on innocuous topics or wire service rewrites requiring only a courtesy call, I pushed hard.

There was another reason I was aggressive. The job enabled me to use my anger toward authority, my antipathy toward anyone who reminded me of the sarge, my lack of respect for the mighty. People like me are not a good fit at most jobs. But in the city room of a newspaper, these are good attributes for a reporter, and they served me well.

Every morning I walked into the city room at 6:00 a.m., an hour before anyone else. In those quiet moments while the beast was slumbering, I walked around the city room, listened to the teletype machines, ran my hands over different typewriters, and imagined the faces of the reporters who sat behind each desk. I leaned against the city editor's desk and looked out over the newsroom, imagining the greatest collection of driven and idealistic people I had ever known sitting behind those desks. I ran my hands over my old Royal typewriter. I felt the latent energy that in an hour would explode into a controlled frenzy. That mood would continue until midafternoon when the Blue Streak went to bed. We on the *Journal* fed the beast during the day, and *Constitution* reporters fed the beast through the night.

A few reporters introduced themselves, but it was quick and pro forma. I was just another unproven newbie in a madras sports coat, khaki pants, white socks, cheap shoes, and an anxious manner. No one had to ask where I was from. They knew I was from somewhere in South Georgia, from *down there*.

Reporters were not known for being well-dressed. And they are still not. They dress like retired military people, that is, there was always something a bit off. Maybe the tie was yesterday's color and had a knot like a hawser. Maybe the white shirt was dingy and the cuffs frayed. Maybe the pants were too short. Maybe the shirt worn with the suit was short-sleeved. Many people laughed and shrugged when they talked of the way reporters dressed. But we did not care. The job was all that mattered.

I had been at the paper about a month when I arrived one morning and heard the insistent ringing of the telephone on the city editor's desk. I was far too junior to answer that phone. I looked around, but no one else was in the city room. I picked up the phone, deepened my voice, and growled, "City desk."

You have no idea how much I enjoyed saying those words.

At the other end was the switchboard operator. She said a Georgia Bureau of Investigation supervisor was on the line, wanting to talk to an editor. Nobody answered at the *Constitution*, so she'd called the *Journal*. "Let me switch him over," she said.

She was gone before I could say, "I'm not an editor." The GBI wanted to speak to an editor. What the hell could I tell him?

I heard a click and a demanding voice. "Hello. Who is this?"

"City desk."

The agent said the GBI was about to raid an illegal liquor still in South DeKalb, and he thought it would be a good story. He was asking that we cover the story because it would make the GBI look good to be seen as crusaders against whiskey stills. Making illegal whiskey is an ancient and revered art in Georgia, an art practiced by generations of irascible Scots-Irish scattered across the South. It was also illegal.

My mind was spinning a hundred miles an hour. Grasping for time, for an idea, I asked, "Can you tell me more?"

He was impatient. "It's a moonshining operation. We have been after these guys for more than a year. I expect to arrest a half-dozen people and pour out several hundred gallons of illegal whiskey. Then we are going to blow the still. Lots of dynamite. We will hold off on the raid if you can send somebody down. Can you do that?"

I was looking around the city room, my mind tumbling, hoping that a real reporter, a real editor, would walk in the door.

"Can you do that?" the GBI agent repeated, this time in a more urgent and demanding tone.

Desperate, I said, "I'll send my best man."

"Good. What's his name?"

"Robert Coram."

"Okay," he said slowly, and I knew he was writing down my name. He gave me instructions on where to meet his agents. "Tell your man to hurry. And you might want to bring a photographer."

The GBI supervisor knew more about this business than I did.

I hung up the phone and let out a long breath. I had never covered a breaking story on deadline. I called photo and asked for a photographer. I called for a staff car. I put on my coat, grabbed a new notebook, extra pens, and was off. As I rushed down the hall, I realized I had, without an editor's approval or direction, assigned myself to a story, brought in a photographer, and ordered up a staff car. If I did not deliver, my ass would be hung out to dry.

When I met the GBI supervisor, I was so anxious my mouth was dry and my hands were shaking. A dozen agents were lounging about wearing boots and camouflage pants. They looked at me with curiosity. When the supervisor gave the order to proceed, I realized they had been waiting on me. They needed this story to be told.

I ran stooped over and trying to be quiet, following the armed agents through the woods. As we approached the still, the supervisor motioned for all of us to get down on our stomachs and creep forward. Now I realized why the agents wore camo and boots.

With a whispered radio call, the supervisor sent his agents crashing through the last few yards of bushes and trees, waving their weapons, and shouting for everyone to put their hands up. The agents arrested a half-dozen good ole boys, cuffed them, and then placed dynamite under the still.

The good ole boys were growling about "revenooers" when the supervisor called, "Fire in the hole." We ducked and hid behind trees as the dynamite blew the still into twisted pipes and shattered barrels. I asked so many questions that the supervisor finally said, "I think you got it all."

Harold Davis narrowed his eyes when he saw me striding down the hall.

"I'm not late," I said. "I've been out on a story."

He stared at me, not speaking, as I told him what had happened. He nodded.

"Did you have a photographer?" he asked.

"Yes, sir. He's pushing the film and said the photos would be up in a few minutes."

He looked up at the big clock on the wall and said, "You got the feature page. I need two hundred words in ten minutes for the final home."

I nodded. I had been writing the story in my head while I was driving back.

"Yes, sir."

"Get on it." As I turned, he said, "Oh." He waited until I whirled around and stood before his desk. "Next time, call the city desk and let us know what you have. Don't spring a story like this on us with no notice." He waved me away.

I did not bother to take off my coat. I sat down, grabbed two sheets of paper and a piece of carbon paper, lined them up, rolled them into the typewriter, typed *Coram* in the top left-hand corner, and *whiskey*—which told the editor what the story was about—in the upper right-hand corner, and began writing.

The feature page did not run every day. But when there was an immediate story with good photos, the paper emphasized the importance of the story by giving it a full page. The copy was short, the pictures were big, and the page always got a lot of attention. To have the feature page was a coup for any reporter.

A few hours later, a copy boy brought a stack of papers to the city room—the first copies off the presses of the final home edition—and distributed them around the city room. Of course, every reporter picked up the paper and scanned it to see how his story was played.

I flipped to the feature page and saw my first byline, and I knew I would never again experience that sense of accomplishment, that sense of pride, that fulfillment. I stared at my byline. I stared at the photos. I read the story. I stared at my byline. I stared at the photos. I read the story. All the time I kept my head in the newspaper, but occasionally, I glanced to the side and scanned the newsroom.

Nobody reads a newspaper the way a reporter does. Or as quickly. Around the newsroom, a few reporters, bewildered expressions on their faces, were looking around the room.

"Who is Robert Coram?" one of them muttered.

A tall, rangy, black-haired man wearing a big smile walked to my desk, stuck out his hand, and said, "You're Robert Coram?"

"Yes."

"John Pennington." He laughed. "You hit the ground running. A really good piece. Tight. It covered everything."

Holy shit. John Pennington was standing by my desk. He was a big man with a dark complexion and bright, intelligent eyes. He was an iconic figure in Georgia journalism and a man whose work I had long admired.

"Welcome to the *Atlanta Journal*," he said.

"Thanks."

John smiled and said, "I have to ask you something. You just went to work here. How did you get a source like that so quickly? Do you know somebody at the GBI?"

I shrugged. "No. I don't know anyone at the GBI. I just came to work early and picked up the phone."

For a moment, he was bewildered. Then he threw his head back, and his laughter was heard all over the newsroom. "You came to work early, and you picked up the phone," he repeated.

John Pennington standing by my desk and laughing and talking to me did more to vault me into acceptance by the newsroom than anything else. John had been nominated for the Pulitzer Prize. He was a star. His investigative pieces caused changes in local or state government. Someone was fired, or a department abolished, or a prison camp was closed. Almost every person in public office in Georgia knew who he was.

"That was good reporting on deadline," John said. "Can you write as well as you can report?"

I paused. I had never made such a distinction. Being a reporter was being a writer. Or so I thought.

"I don't know."

"Where you from?"

"Edison, down in—"

"I know where Edison is," he interrupted. "That's not far from—"

"I know," I interrupted.

"You met everyone in the newsroom?"

"A few."

"Well, you are about to meet them all. Come with me." We walked from desk to desk, John introducing me to everyone and often repeating, "He got that story today because he came to work early and picked up the phone." Every time he said it, he laughed.

Two of the people I met were new reporters, guys who had come to work here within a few days of when I was hired. One of them shook his head and smiled when we were introduced. "I saw your piece. You are a lucky son of a bitch."

John laughed. "All you have to do is come to work early and pick up the phone."

After we had stopped at every desk, John invited me to lunch. With a smile, he said he would get me back before the Blue Streak deadline in case I got another phone call. He laughed and shook his head. "I love what you did."

In the coming weeks, I did more. The feature page story moved me up a notch in the newsroom, and the city desk let me write book reviews, op-ed pieces, features, and news stories. A day without a byline was like a day without food. At last, I was doing what I wanted to do. I was a reporter for the Atlanta papers. There was no higher calling.

18

For Georgia politicians in the 1960s, the city room of the *Atlanta Journal* was a combination of Lourdes and the Ganges: a place where miracles could happen, where the lame could be made to walk and the blind to see. And where the crooked could be made straight.

For a political candidate in Georgia, the first rule of politicking was: get the newspaper on your side. Failing that, pray the newspapers do not endorse your opponent.

Those who wanted to be elected or to stay elected came to the paper as supplicants. They paid obeisance to the editor, the editorial staff, to the political reporters, and—out of fear—to John Pennington. Then, just to make sure they had covered all bases, they shook hands with every person in the city room, including copy boys.

The governor did not go to the bathroom without checking in with the paper. Many times, I saw him hurrying down the hall, accompanied by a state trooper. He knew the way to the editor's office.

On election nights, the newsroom was the center of the universe. Election Central. Candidates, political hangers-on, reporters, office holders, television reporters—all gathered in the newsroom. We had more information than anyone else. Our election coverage was the basis for almost all media coverage.

Many low-grade rascals inhabited public office in Georgia. As a rule, they were cunning rather than bright, avaricious rather than honest, and most of them believed the purpose of holding public office was to build a mini-kingdom, to appoint their relatives and friends to government jobs, and to steal as much money as they could.

These were the people who, when they did not get the endorsement of the paper, campaigned against the paper. The phrase "them lyin' 'lanna newspapers" was often heard in the hinterlands of Georgia. The paper, and all of us who worked there, were publicly referred to as "Communists" and "nigger lovers" and "left-wingers." We wore those epithets with pride.

Those who cursed us were the most avid readers of the paper. They might not like what they read, but they respected us and knew we could not be threatened away from a story or bought off from a story. If a politician was a brigand or a thief or a bully, we wrote stories that often got them thrown out of office and sometimes thrown into jail.

The power of the paper was not limited to politics. Columnist Paul Hemphill sat at the desk next to mine. He wrote several columns about an unknown bar named Manuel's Tavern and its curmudgeonly owner, Manuel Maloof. Paul's columns made the tavern the most popular bar in Atlanta for politicians, print journalists (TV people knew to stay away), Emory professors, cops, blue-collar workers, lawyers, and people who wanted to gawk at everyone else. Democratic presidential candidates and Democratic gubernatorial candidates always made a campaign stop at Manuel's. Paul's columns gave Manuel Maloof such recognition that he was elected county commissioner.

The papers dictated the assignments of TV reporters. At every press conference, every trial, every political gathering, TV reporters stood there with combed hair, shiny shoes, makeup caked on their faces . . . reading our clips. The TV reporters, whatever they were, were not news people. Not one of them was a real reporter.

After reading a newspaper story a final time, the TV people lowered their voices, wrinkled their brows, made dramatic gestures, and leaned forward with intense looks and talked to the camera as if they knew what they were talking about. We looked upon them with utter contempt. We did not know enough to be afraid of them. We did not realize that television, in a few more years, would become the dominant news medium and that newspaper people would become an endangered species. All we knew was that TV people used hairspray and made more money than we did.

At news conferences, we walked in front of their cameras. We talked over their standups. Often a newspaper reporter had a clicker in his pocket. The clicker was a small metal device that, when pressed, emitted a loud click. When released, another click. The newspaper reporter clicked through the important parts of every news conference. In the hubbub of a news conference, few people noticed. But when TV people returned to the studio and began processing their tape, the clicks were audible. We fouled up many news conferences.

In the 1960s, radio as a news medium was fading into insignificance. Atlanta had one radio reporter who could chop the wood: Aubrey Morris, who worked for WSB Radio. He had a twangy drawl that made every listener wonder how the hell he ever got a job in radio. But Aubrey had many scoops under his belt, the best known of which occurred when the king of a Middle Eastern country visited Atlanta. Security was tight. When the king's airplane landed, news people were kept a hundred yards away behind a fence. The aircraft boarding platform was pushed across the tarmac. When the aircraft door opened and the king stepped out, Aubrey jumped out of hiding, ran up the ramp, pushed his microphone in the king's face, and said, "King, what do you think of Atlanta?"

The nonplussed king said he had no thoughts on the matter. "Well, if you did have any thoughts, what would they be?" Aubrey asked.

Aubrey was a newshound. We respected him.

With television not yet a factor, radio a fading medium, and the wire services oriented toward a national audience, Atlanta newspapers were the most significant statewide news outlet in Georgia. Their influence spread across the South.

We newspaper people were more than a little aloof. We ran no polls and did not care if we were vilified. When someone asked how we decided what news was, we said, "News is whatever the city editor says it is." If someone called to complain about a story, we listened. But unless there was a factual error, we paid them no attention. We became hardened. We became rude. We became defensive. We became arrogant. We built a shield to deflect people who wanted their daughter's graduation notice in the paper, or a story about winning a bridge tournament, or a story about a vacation to Europe. We did not believe the paper was a bulletin board, and we did not believe in community outreach. We did not ask people what they wanted to read. We told people what they needed to know. And circulation kept growing.

Few businesses have as many characters as did newspapers. We shook our heads at the oddballs, but we revered them.

One editor had false teeth and on a tight deadline would thrust out his upper plate and show what appeared to be the world's greatest overbite. Then he would suck his upper plate back in. His teeth clicked and slurped in a wet click. In and out. In and out as he edited copy with speed and with care.

And there was the news editor who may have originated the three-martini lunch. Every day after lunch, we locked him in his office until late in the day when someone would drive him home. He sat in his office all afternoon talking to himself.

Another columnist always left his hat and glasses on his desk. We would walk by his office and through the glass wall would see the hat and glasses and know he was somewhere in the building. But he had an extra hat and glasses to leave on his desk while he wandered God knows where.

I was young and idealistic and passionate about my work. I was full of myself and had more than a little self-righteousness. I was an aggressive reporter and, I think, a good reporter.

Everything about being a newspaperman fed my insecurities, my sense of being an outsider, of not belonging. Reporters never join anything but the church. Being an outsider fit my nature. It compensated for my coming from a small nowhere town in southwest Georgia. It caused my defiance toward authority to bloom.

About a month after my feature page on the illegal whiskey still, the city editor made me a beat reporter covering Clayton and Cobb counties. Having a beat freed me from the city desk. The first thing a beat reporter learns is that if he comes up with enough stories to feed the beast, the city editors will stay off his ass. Insecure editors sometimes come up with stupid story ideas; good city editors let us find the stories.

I was the first reporter to have these two counties as a beat. They were on opposite sides of Atlanta, both outside the Perimeter Highway, and both led by public officials so venal and incompetent that writing of their misdeeds was like picking low-hanging fruit. In the beginning, elected officials in these two counties thought it a great honor to have a reporter from the Atlanta papers covering them on a regular basis. A month later, they thought a biblical plague had been visited upon them.

I wrote stories that resulted in the mayor and the entire city council of Forest Park, a town in Clayton County, being tossed out of office. The mayor and his friends had floated a bond issue to build a city recreation center. The roof was so low that if a diver bounced on the diving board, he banged his head against the roof.

I wrote stories that changed the design of a major highway in Cobb County. Local officials had bought land along the road and wanted the road to be unlimited access. They wanted to have numerous intersections built so they could build gas stations and convenience stores on each corner. My stories made the state highway department put up a fence along the road and declare it limited access.

I was indefatigable in searching out and digging for what we called initiative stories or enterprise pieces. These stories often wound up in the Sunday paper: stories about spending twenty-four hours in the bus station, a night at the Atlanta airport, scuba diving in an abandoned quarry, and the tranquility of the north Georgia mountains.

But I liked hard news stories best. I found that having a beat and developing sources was like having a garden. Some sources, like some plants, needed tender loving care. Others thrived on nothing but a ray of sunshine and an occasional bit of water. Others needed a lot of fertilizer to be heaped upon them. I developed new sources and took care of them. I found that plants growing in the far corners of the garden could bear the best fruit, that secretaries or low-level bureaucrats could be better sources than their elected bosses. A little manure heaped on them, and they flowered.

Everyone who provides information to a newspaper reporter has a reason. He has an agenda. I don't care about the reason or the agenda as long as the information is solid.

Having a beat meant covering breaking stories. And breaking stories needed a new lede for every edition. The first time I picked up a phone and dictated a breaking story, I was so anxious that I found it difficult to speak. I stumbled and stuttered and backed up and went sideways. But the editor on the other end of the phone was a kind and patient man, and he walked me through the story, making suggestions, leading me. After a few more efforts, dictating a story was second nature. I could flip the pages in my notebook, pick out the lede, and develop the story in my mind. Soon dictating a story became second nature. I could dictate a breaking story on deadline, talking as fast as the typist back at the paper could type. And I could add a new lede for every addition.

I don't think I was ever as proud of an accomplishment as I was in dictating breaking stories under deadline, knowing that back in the city room, every paragraph was ripped from a typewriter, sent to an editor, to the copy desk, and to the composing room. I was building a story block by block, and the pieces had to fit together in a seamless and logical fashion. And when I finished the story, I should exit with a powerful kicker.

Superior court judges in Clayton and Cobb counties were pleased to have an Atlanta reporter cover their trials. Judges, like all public officials, like to see their names in the paper. One judge reserved the aisle seat on the front bench in his courtroom for me. And if, during a trial, I looked at him and tapped my watch, he called a recess so I could go out in the hall to a pay phone and dictate a new lede. Soon the judge knew my deadlines and as the time approached would look at me with raised eyebrows. If I nodded, he declared a recess. And while I was out of the courtroom, a bailiff guarded my front row seat. When I finished dictating a new lede and reentered the courtroom, I nodded toward a bailiff, who went into the judge's chambers and told him I was back in the front row and we could resume the trial.

Being a reporter for the Atlanta papers was a heady experience indeed.

ONE day, John Pennington came to work, and I noticed he had not shaved. John had black hair and dark skin and within three weeks had grown a thick bushy beard.

We knew John was onto a big story, one that required him to disguise his appearance. Elected officials read the half-page promotional ads the paper ran about John; they knew what he looked like. And we knew not to ask John what he was working on.

Then one day, John did not show up for work. Several weeks later when he returned and walked into the city room, he was clean-shaven and carrying a thick sheaf of typing paper.

John had taken his wife and three children, rented a car with New Jersey license plates, and driven along US 17 in coastal McIntosh County in deep southeast Georgia. In those pre-interstate days, US 17 was the main north-south road for people from the north going to Florida in the fall and returning in the spring. In McIntosh, every hundred yards or so was either a brothel, a gambling joint, a clip joint, or a service station where—when the attendant checked the oil—he would disable something that, to repair, cost an exorbitant sum. Payable in cash. No cash, no car. And if the owner complained, a sheriff's deputy threatened to send him to jail.

Cars with out-of-state tags often were charged with speeding. The officer who stopped the car demanded cash. Again, cash or jail.

The sheriff of McIntosh County, as were many Georgia sheriffs of the time, was the most powerful elected official in the county. Called the high sheriff, he answered to no one except the voters. And the powerful sheriffs in rural counties were not intimidated by an Atlanta reporter.

In McIntosh, the sheriff was like a mafia don; he controlled every illegal operation. The sheriff was so bold that when the US military handed over a local WWII air base to the county, the sheriff turned it into one big gambling den and brothel. And there were many stories—some of them true—about people who ran afoul of the sheriff and were tossed to the alligators.

That's where John was going. To McIntosh County, where he and his family would pretend to be tourists from New Jersey. As everyone knows, those are the worst kinds of tourists.

John's primary source was the owner and publisher of a weekly newspaper in the county, the *Darien News*. The editor knew everything going on in the county. But his office had been set afire, and shots had been fired into his windows. He got the message and did not write of county events. But he called John and told him every detail of every event, and then John wrote the stories, and the local editor did a piece about what the lying Atlanta newspapers had said about this idyllic little county.

John's series of stories were the first to expose the systemic corruption in McIntosh County. The public outcry forced the governor of Georgia to take actions to begin to clean up the county. But the sheriff was so politically powerful that the governor was afraid to push too hard. And it would be another decade before the county became semirespectable. John's stories influenced a successful book titled *Praying for Sheetrock* by Melissa Faye Greene.

I pressed John for details about the research for his series. My admiration for him grew, as did my desire to be an investigative reporter.

John knew I idolized him. He counseled me, gave me advice, and sometimes—on a big story when the presence of two reporters was required—he took me along on his reporting trips. On many trips, John and I flew in a small Cessna.

John was the first private pilot I had ever known.

After John did a story about a middle Georgia sheriff's felonious nincompoopery—which, again, involved preying on tourists. The GBI investigated the sheriff. Now the sheriff was facing possible indictment, and he was angry as a kicked bear. He put out the word that he knew John Pennington was the reason for all his problems, and if that Atlanta newspaper guy ever came back to his county, the sheriff was going to beat the hell out of him, put him in jail, and throw away the key.

Someone called John and told him of the threat. John hung up the phone and shouted across the newsroom, "Hey, Robert, want to fly to South Georgia with me and watch a sheriff kick my butt?"

The next morning, John and I took off from Fulton County Airport in a Cessna 152, a tiny two-seat, training aircraft. The rental rate was such that John could file an expense report for the mileage and just about break even.

The little aircraft cruised at maybe a hundred miles per hour. At thirty-five hundred feet, every thermal bounced us about. During the flight, John gave me a cram course in flying and let me handle the aircraft.

Once in Cordele, we rented a car and drove to the sheriff's office. John walked through the door with a big smile, and with his booming voice announced, "My name is John Pennington, and I'm here to see the sheriff. I understand he is looking for me."

A half-dozen deputies were lounging around, hands on their cantilevered bellies, trying to remember when it was they had last seen their toes. They were like indolent lions, lazy but eyes alert, waiting to pounce on a hapless prey. Every deputy froze, looked at John, looked at me, then looked again at John.

After maybe ten seconds, the deputy with the biggest stomach, a man who had not seen his toes in five years, introduced himself as the chief deputy and said the sheriff had gone to the courthouse to visit the county clerk.

"Thanks," John said. "I'll catch up with him there." He turned to leave.

"Mr. Pennington, you sure you want to do that?" the chief deputy asked in a tone that was almost threatening.

John stopped, turned, and stared at the chief deputy. "Yes, I am sure. Why do you ask?"

The chief deputy tried to stare John down. But John Pennington was not some hapless out-of-state tourist frightened at the thought of driving through the Deep South. Nor was he a local farmer who acknowledged the sheriff as a minor deity. Nor was he some local piece of white trash caught in a minor infraction and playing at obeisance to a tyrannical deputy. No. He was John Pennington of the *Atlanta Journal*, and he could walk through the valley of the shadow of death and fear no evil. His typewriter was more powerful than the sheriff's pistol, his certitude more powerful than the sheriff's uniform, and his moral authority greater than the sheriff's venality.

It was a one-sided battle. And when the deputy broke his stare, in an effort to save face, he said, "Mr. Pennington, you know what the sheriff said about you?"

"Yes. And I want to give him a chance to live up to his word." John pointed to the radio atop the desk and said, "Call him on that thing and tell him I am on the way."

Without waiting for an answer, he motioned for me to follow. As we went out the door, the chief deputy, given bravado by the sight of John's back, said, "Mr. Pennington, you can count on it."

In the car, I said, "John, aren't you nervous about this?"

John threw back his head and laughed. "The man is a crook," he said. "He has violated his oath of office. He is preying on tourists. He is not supposed to collect cash from a speeder. He is supposed to give the violator a ticket and have him come to court. A judge decides if he is guilty, if he should pay a fine, and, if so, how much."

"Yeah, but—"

"Robert, don't ever be afraid of a crook. Not many of them are dumb enough to do anything to an Atlanta reporter." He laughed. "But if this one does attack me, you take notes. You get to write the story." He threw back his head and laughed with the joy of combat.

I was a half step behind John when we entered the courthouse, walked down the long dark hall whose walls were flecked with peeling green paint, and whose floors were of dark heart pine. On either side were plain black doors, the bottom half wood and the top half frosted glass. The name and title of the inhabitant were painted on the glass. A courthouse smell pervaded the air, the smell of cleaning fluids, wax, sweat, fear.

John pushed open a door that announced *Clerk of Superior Court*. The clerk was a middle-aged woman with dark hair and eyes that had seen everything. "You're John Pennington," she said. She looked at John, looked at me, looked back at John and said, "You gonna need somebody a lot bigger than that if the sheriff sees you."

John's eyes sparkled. "That's who I am looking for. The deputies said he was in the courthouse. Have you seen him?"

The clerk made no effort to hide her surprise. "*You* are looking for the sheriff?" She snorted. "You better hope you don't find him."

"Is he in the courthouse?" John asked.

She bent toward her desk, picked up a pencil, and waved her hand, dismissing us from her office.

We never found the sheriff that day, only people who said he had just been there and we better hope we did not find him because he was angry. That afternoon we flew back to Atlanta, and John wrote a piece rehashing his earlier stories about the sheriff and saying the sheriff had threatened him but was not available when John went looking for him. It was a piece that would humiliate the sheriff in front of his deputies and his constituents.

As he began writing the piece, he asked me to look over his shoulder and make suggestions. When he handed the piece to the city editor, he said, "Joint byline. Add Robert's name."

As did almost everything John wrote, the piece appeared on the front page. When the first copies off the press were passed around the city room, one of the other young reporters who sat two desks away from me and who had been writing obits for months glanced at the front page, saw that I had a joint byline with John Pennington, and said, "Coram, you are a lucky son of a bitch."

I had heard that before.

As I looked at the two bylines, I recalled the satisfaction, even the exultation, I had felt at my first byline, the story about the whiskey still. Sharing a byline with John Pennington was better.

A few years later, a no-name peanut farmer in deep southwest Georgia ran for the local school board. The incumbent and the local political bosses rigged the election so that their man, and not the no-name farmer, won the election. The no-name farmer was appalled at the raw corrupt power he had faced and called his cousin, who was an assistant city editor on the *Journal*. The assistant city editor told John to go down and check out the election. John's subsequent stories broke up the long-lasting political cabal in the county, sent several people to jail, and forced a new election in which the peanut farmer won. The farmer brought the school board into the twentieth century and gave him the platform to run for governor of Georgia. His name was Jimmy Carter, and he would remain John's lifelong friend. After Carter became president in the late 1970s, he often said he would not be president had it not been for John Pennington.

That's what it was like to be a reporter for a major metropolitan daily at that time and at that place. Newspapers swept everything before them. Contrary to everything the sarge had ever told me, I *had* amounted to something. I had a great job. I was doing work that made a difference. John Pennington was my mentor and my hero.

But I did not have John's experience and John's judgment.

19

ONE morning, I told Leslie I wanted to take flying lessons.

She looked at me, bewildered, and said we have been talking about learning to sail and then maybe buying a small sailboat. She wanted to find something we could do together. Flying lessons were expensive. She paused and said we couldn't do both.

She was right. My newspaper salary and her secretary salary—she had moved to a job at a local radio station—were not enough.

I agreed that lessons were expensive but said I would space out the lessons for minimum impact on our budget. And once I got my license, we could fly around the country, maybe even to the Bahamas. I said I would write freelance stories about our trips, and every expense would be deductible from our taxes.

She said we had to spend the money before we could deduct it. She asked if we could afford the lessons. I shrugged. Details.

She said we needed a sofa. Could we buy a sofa before I began flying lessons?

Again, she was right. I had rigged a sofa by varnishing a door, putting metal legs on it, then placing cushions on top. To me, it was functional, even if the cushions slid out from under a person's behind and the back cushions slid down the wall. To Leslie, it belonged in a college dorm. But I said nothing was wrong with our sofa.

"If you really want to take flying lessons . . ." Her voice trailed off.

"I do."

"Okay. But let's begin putting money aside for a sofa."

I soloed in eight hours and then set about building up the forty hours necessary to get my private license. Months later, I got my license, came home, and said, "Let's go somewhere this weekend."

"Where do you want to go?"

"How about Cumberland Island? There is a dirt runway there. We can stay at Grayfield Inn, and they will let us have a truck to drive to the beach."

"Have you already planned this?"

"I called them. They have a vacancy."

"Isn't it expensive?"

"It's only two nights. We can have a great time on the beach. The weather forecast is for clear weather."

"Do we have the money?"

"I moved some money around. We can do it."

Her lips tightened. "You took the money we were saving to buy a sofa?"

"We can put it back. You will love being on the beach."

She did not speak for a long moment. And in the silence, she saw her sofa pushed even further into the background.

On Friday, we made the two-hour flight to Cumberland, me not realizing how selfish and profligate I was and thinking how dashing and glamorous it was to rent an airplane and fly to the Georgia coast and stay in a famous inn. Everything about this weekend was a long way from Edison.

That weekend, I think Leslie had as good a time as she could allow herself to have.

But she was quiet on the return flight.

HAROLD Davis decided to go to graduate school and join the public affairs office for Georgia State College. John Pennington would be the new city editor. Harold thought I was too aggressive, not gentlemanly enough, and he feared I might press too hard in interviewing a public official on stories that were not all that important. As a gift to John, he wanted to fire me before he went off to become a flack.

John said that he was not going to fire me; he was going to promote me. The first staff change he made was to assign me to the Fulton County Courthouse, one of the most prestigious beats on the paper. Atlanta is located in Fulton County, and much of what happened in the courthouse was of interest throughout the metropolitan area.

"Monday go over there and look around and meet people," John said. "It will take you a few days to get your feet on the ground. Don't worry about getting a story for the first few days."

Monday, I was at the courthouse before 7:00 a.m., hanging out in the cafeteria where elected officials and staff had breakfast or coffee. I went from table to table meeting everyone, focusing on low- and midlevel employees, plants that prefer dark corners. I went from department head to department head, introducing myself and telling them I was the *Journal*'s new courthouse reporter. Several of them, eager to have a good start with the new reporter, gave me a rundown of their department's activities, some of which had not been made public.

At the end of the day, I stopped by the city desk and said I would have five stories for tomorrow's first edition, a quick synopsis of each, and an estimated word count.

John raised his eyebrows, looked at me, and said, "Wasn't today your first day at the courthouse?"

"It was."

He tilted back his head and laughed, delighted to know his judgment had proven to be correct. And I was delighted that I had pleased John. Not only did I want him to think well of me, I wanted to beat the *Constitution* on every story, and I wanted to do initiative stories that would keep my paper ahead of the *Constitution*. The *Constitution* was my bitter enemy, and *Constitution* reporters were to be run over and savaged and humiliated at every opportunity.

I did not get a good start on this goal. And that was because of Reuben Smith, the *Constitution*'s courthouse reporter.

Reuben was a tall, laconic man about my age, a chain-smoker and an irreverent man with a caustic sense of humor. He had been covering the courthouse for six months and was a formidable reporter and a ruthless competitor.

The courthouse pressroom was a nook in a back corner on the third floor. Inside was room for two desks and a tatty couch. The room had no windows. Across the glass door was the *Atlanta Constitution*. A typewriter, a phone, and stacks of typing paper and carbon paper sat atop each desk.

Reuben handed me a key to the room. "The *Journal* and the *Constitution* are the only people allowed in here," he said. "Never let a TV person in here." He shrugged. "I'll have the courthouse maintenance guy paint the name of your paper on the door."

"Why isn't it there already? We have always had a reporter here."

Reuben smiled, took a long puff from his cigarette, and blew a cloud of smoke toward me. "I didn't like the last son of a bitch the *Journal* sent over here." He grinned a satisfied grin. "He didn't have a key to the office."

"Why not?"

"I told the county manager I would make it my life's work to look under every rock I could find and write nothing but negative stories about the county unless he changed the locks and not give one to the *Journal* guy."

I stared. I had never shared a beat with a *Constitution* reporter. This was a blood sport.

"Why do I get a key?"

He shrugged. "I'm willing to give you a chance." His mouth smiled, but his eyes were cold.

Reuben roamed the courthouse in the morning and wrote his stories in the afternoon. When his day ended, he took the original copy back to his city editor. If he called in a breaking story, he wrote it first, then dictated from his copy. The carbons he kept in a basket atop his desk. My mornings were frantic as I had deadlines every few hours. And sometimes when Reuben was out of the office, I riffled through his carbons to see what he was working on.

Reuben and I might sometimes be in the room together, but for most of the day, we stayed out of each other's sight. We held our initiative stories close until after the other person's deadlines had passed.

Late one morning, Reuben rushed into the press office, sat behind his desk, and began typing.

"What's going on?" I asked as if I did not care.

He turned to look at me, lit a cigarette, tilted his head back so the smoke would not get in his eyes, and laughed. "You think I'm going to tell you?"

If Reuben published a story that I should have had in my paper first, my humiliation would be great. *Journal* reporters would sidle up to my desk and say, "Did you see that story Reuben Smith had?"

Reuben returned to his staccato two-fingered typing. "This one can't wait. I've got to get this to the city desk. There is some back-story they need to know about."

He continued typing while I made a few phone calls to county officials, keeping my voice low so Reuben could not hear me.

After maybe fifteen minutes, Reuben stood up, collected the original copies of his story, stacked the carbons in a wire basket atop his desk, grabbed his coat, and was gone.

I waited a couple of minutes to make sure he had not forgotten something and was returning to the office. I sidled over to his desk, leaned over, and read the first page of the story he had just written. My eyes widened. I picked up the first page, glanced toward the door, and read the second page. With each sentence, I became more anxious.

Reuben's story was about Superior Court Judge Durwood Pye, a hatchet-faced man so cranky and irritable and so dismissive of the Atlanta papers that he had once ordered a photographer not to set foot on the city block where the courthouse was located. He was not afraid of the Atlanta papers and was willing to prove that he had more power than did the papers. Everyone who dealt with Judge Pye, including lawyers, showed him great deference. When Judge Pye was on the bench, his eyes darted about the courtroom looking for someone upon whom he could vent his bile. He had tossed witnesses out of his courtroom for chewing gum or whispering to a companion.

Editors at both papers were always on the lookout for a story that might embarrass the judge. It was a careful and cautious search because should they publish a story and the judge caught them, it would be a great embarrassment for the paper. Nevertheless, the search continued.

Reuben's story said that when a young Muslim man came to Judge Pye's courtroom wearing a knitted cap, the judge ordered him to either take off or to leave the courtroom. The young man stood up, said his cap was required by his faith, and he would not take it off. Furthermore, a courtroom was a public place, and he was not leaving. The judge reeled at such temerity, berated the young man, and ordered two bailiffs to eject him from the courtroom. Reuben had strong quotes from both the young man and the judge.

This was a front-page story, and it had happened on my time, on my deadline. I looked at my watch. If I hurried and confirmed the story, I could get it into both the final home and the Blue Streak. The latter was sold on the street and read by thousands as commuters went home from work.

I read Reuben's story again to cement the details in my mind, grabbed my notebook, straightened my tie, buttoned my coat, opened the door, and rushed down the hall. The judge was not in his chambers. His secretary, a stern and steely middle-aged woman, was surprised that a reporter would seek out the judge. She eyed me as if I were a laboratory specimen. "The judge is on the bench," she said. Translated, that meant, "The king is on his throne."

Not good. I walked out of the office and back down the hall to the door of the courtroom. I sighed took a deep breath and entered. I walked down the center aisle and stood between the assistant district attorney and the defense attorney, both of whom turned and stared at me as if I had taken leave of my senses. The judge narrowed his eyes and leaned back in his chair. The judge scared me more than my daddy used to scare me. But I was a reporter, and I was on the job. I raised my notebook in the air to get the judge's attention.

"Why are you standing up in my courtroom?" the judge growled. "Why are you waving? What is the matter with you?"

In my most diffident voice, I said, "Your Honor, I apologize for interrupting the court. But I'm on a deadline and wondered if I might have a quick word with you."

To my left and to my right, the lawyers moved farther away.

The judge bowed up so fast that for a moment I wondered if he had some sort of air compressor under his robe. He almost doubled in size, he was so outraged. When he spoke, his voice cut like a knife. "I am in the middle of a trial, and your deadline is irrelevant. I—"

I compounded my sins by interrupting the judge. "Your Honor, can you confirm that you threw a Muslim man out of your courtroom because he would not take off his cap?"

The judge stared at me in utter disbelief. I could hear his teeth grinding. He paused to control his anger. "Bailiff," he said. A beefy uniformed officer appeared beside me, looking at the judge, awaiting his orders. I had visions of being tossed into the county jail.

The judge labored to get control of himself. "Young man, you clearly are not in possession of your faculties. Were it not for the fact you have demonstrated that you are intellectually handicapped, I would order you remanded to the county jail."

The bailiff nudged me. But the judge wasn't waiting for a response. "Bailiff, remove this person from my courtroom. And he is not to return. Not today or any other day. Nor is he allowed in my office. I will write an order to that effect."

The bailiff turned me around and frog-walked me to the door. "Boy, you done got on the judge's bad side," he whispered. Knowing the judge was watching, he pushed me through the door, followed me, and stood in front of the closed door. "You making stuff up," he said in a bewildered voice. "Judge ain't throwed nobody out of his courtroom." He smiled. "Except you."

I was a shaken young man as I walked down the hall and unlocked the door of the press room. Reuben was leaning back in his chair, feet atop his desk, a big smile on his face. "You get a good interview with Judge Pye?" He laughed and took a puff off his cigarette.

I thought Reuben had returned to the paper. Why was he here? It took me a moment to understand. "You son of a bitch. You set me up."

"What happened?"

"He threw me out of his courtroom. Threatened to jail me for contempt. You sneaky bastard."

Reuben smiled and blew a smoke ring toward me. He was pleased with himself. "Keep your hands off my carbons," he said.

I did.

20

In the 1960s, Ralph McGill was the best-known newspaperman in America. National publications called him "the conscience of the South." He was a confidante of presidents and heads of state and a much-desired speaker all across the country. Always, he spoke of the gathering racial storm. His syndicated column was the best-read part of newspapers in many states. He was as loved and revered by journalists as he was hated and reviled by racists.

Reporters admired McGill because he had won a Pulitzer in 1959 and because he was the most professional newsman we knew. He knocked out a 750-word column seven days a week, 5,250 words a week. He traveled the world, but his column was always at column one, page one in the *Constitution*. He never missed a day. We heard that when he was traveling, he would sometimes sit down with his battered old Royal and knock out three columns.

McGill was guided by his own lights, not by the turbulent wake of segregationists (we called them "segs") who painted him as the antichrist and a Communist and called him "Rastus McGill." Racists live in both the North and the South. But no one knows how to hate the way a Southern racist hates. The hate of a Southerner is base and vile and mean and irrational. It exists in the marrow of the bones and rarely can be turned around.

From time to time, I saw McGill leaving the building for lunch. He always smiled and nodded but seemed to be thinking of big events. When he returned from lunch, he often was accompanied by Gene Patterson, editor of the *Constitution*, and Harold Martin, a *Constitution* columnist.

McGill, whom people on the paper called "Pappy," was about five feet eight inches tall, pudgy, avuncular, and with eyes that could see over the hill. Patterson was about the same height but walked with shoulders back and chest forward. He had been a tank commander in Patton's army in World War II and had more command presence than any newspaper person I have ever seen. Emerson was a big man and tall who towered over his two companions.

Seeing these three men return from lunch, often arm in arm and laughing uproariously, fulfilled my ideas of what great journalists did at lunch.

In April 1963, Attorney General Robert Kennedy was in Atlanta and popped in unannounced to see McGill. Pappy was out, so Kennedy wrote him an affectionate note and left it on his desk. McGill was that sort of man.

A few months later, Pappy published a book titled *The South and the Southerner*. National publications swooned over the book. I bought the book. After I read it, I held it in my lap and ran my hands over it, awed by the knowledge that I owed a book written by Ralph McGill.

I brought the book to the office, showed it to John Pennington, and asked, "Do you think Mr. McGill would sign this if I took it up to his office?"

John was editing a piece of copy and mumbled something to the effect that, yes, McGill would sign the book, and I should call McGill's secretary and tell her I wanted to come upstairs to visit Pappy.

I looked doubtful. John smiled, picked up the phone, dialed an extension and said, "Grace, do you recognize my golden voice?" He paused, laughed, and said, "One of my reporters has a copy of Pappy's book and wants to come up and get it signed. Is he in?"

After a long moment, he said, "Thanks, Grace," and hung up. He went back to the story he was editing, jerked his thumb toward the elevators, and said, "Pappy is waiting for you."

I shook my head. The idea of seeing McGill in his office was intimidating. As a reporter, I had met a governor, the mayor, congressmen, and CEOs of the biggest companies in Atlanta. But this was *McGill*, a man who was a legend when I was a boy.

I looked down at the book in my hands and said I had planned to leave it with his secretary and pick it up later.

John did not look up. "He. Is. In. His. Office. Waiting." Again, he jerked his thumb toward the elevators.

Even though the *Constitution* and the *Journal* were sister papers and in the same building and had the same owner, there was a world of separation between the two papers. When we reporters told outsiders about how we loved to beat the *Constitution*, they did not believe us. The public saw the two papers as one and could not accept the idea that the two newsrooms fought every day. When I stepped off the elevators on the sixth floor, it was my first visit to the *Constitution*. I was in an enemy camp.

In addition to my being intimidated by McGill, there was another reason for my being wobbly: McGill had written a book. That placed him at the apex of the writing business. I was beginning to sense a sort of progression in writing. First, one became a newspaper reporter and learned certain basic skills: sorting through an enormous amount of data, finding the core essence of that data, and writing about it with quick and clear prose. Then one wrote for magazines and learned that a three-thousand-word piece required a different skillset set than did writing for a newspaper. After writing for magazines, one wrote books. The Great American Novel was the goal, but nonfiction was good. Thus, McGill sat atop the pyramid I wanted to climb.

Grace looked up and smiled when I entered her office. She was a gray-haired woman, as elegant in dress and demeanor as she was in manners. "Robert," she said as if we were long-time friends. "Do come in."

I held up McGill's book. No matter what John Pennington had told me, I expected her to ask me to leave the book on her desk, she would have McGill sign it, and a copy boy would return it to me. A young *Journal* reporter did not schmooze with McGill.

Grace smiled, nodded toward Pappy's office, and gently said, "It is okay. He wants you to come in."

McGill stood up when I entered his vast and cluttered office. He stuck out his hand. "Robert, I've been wanting to meet you." He named several stories I had written in recent weeks, talked of specific details in those stories, and said, "Good work. Good work." He shrugged ruefully. "Several of those were on our time."

"Thank you, sir." We shook hands. He pointed toward a wooden straight-back chair that sat behind his desk alongside his own chair. "Sit here. Let's talk for a while." He looked at me and said, "I'm not keeping you from your deadline, am I?"

"Oh, no, sir." Dazed, I held up his book. "I bought your book." I held it out toward him.

He took it, looked at the cover, and shook his head. "You know, I never liked this title. But I couldn't come up with anything better, so I had to let it stand."

What could I say? He was revealing secrets from the world of publishing, and I was a young reporter. I shrugged in sympathy and looked around. A bookcase stretched the length of one wall. A wasp nest dangled from a bookshelf. Several front pages from the *Thunderbolt*, a seg tabloid out of Augusta, were framed and hanging on the wall. Each excoriated McGill. McGill knew how to piss people off. It was not deliberate, just as his ability to generate respect and veneration was not deliberate.

There was a photo of McGill with John F. Kennedy, another of him with Lyndon B. Johnson. Several other people I recognized but did not know their names. Papers were scattered across McGill's desk.

Most details of my half-hour conversation with Pappy McGill, I do not remember. His comments ranged from events in Europe to inside gossip about LBJ and how the South was ripping itself to pieces over civil rights. He said the South was unable to do the right thing, unable to do anything but once again pick a losing cause.

All I remember about my response is "Yes, sir." McGill must have thought the *Journal* hired village idiots as reporters.

Several times the phone on McGill's desk rang. Each time, without breaking eye contact with me, he said, "Grace, would you get that please?" She did, and I sensed from her voice she was talking with important people when she said, "Mr. McGill is in a meeting. May I have him return your call?"

After about a half hour, McGill picked up his book again and said, "Let me sign this for you. I know you *Journal* reporters have lots of deadlines, and I don't want to keep you from your work."

He opened the book to the title page and wrote, *To Robert Coram, with my best wishes and my hopes that he will have a fine career.*

For the rest of my life, I would treasure that book. I knew where it was on my bookcase, and often, in the years ahead, I would pull it down, read the inscription, and think of that morning when I sat with Pappy McGill. In my career, I would interview many famous people. If I remember them, the memories are dim. But I remember the half hour I spent with Pappy McGill.

21

THE *Journal* and the *Constitution* published a combined edition on Sunday—a five-pounder that went to more than a half-million readers. Reporters know, deep in their hearts, they are not working for salaries; they are working for bylines. And a front-page byline in the Sunday paper was to visit that place where earth and heaven overlap. A front-page byline on Sunday put a smile on a reporter's face for a week.

The *Journal* published the Sunday paper. The midruns—the various sections of the paper—were put to bed by Thursday. Two sections remained open for the Sunday paper: the sports pages and the A section. In the newsroom, we ignored the sports people. They were a lesser species. The A section was all that mattered, and most of the A section was finished by Saturday afternoon. One reporter and an assistant city editor were the city room staff from 4:00 p.m. Saturday until midnight. Most often it was a slow and easy shift, a caretaker job. Only a big breaking local story, one that called for an expensive replate, would send us into action.

I often volunteered for the Saturday shift as it gave me several hours to catch up on my studies from Georgia State.

In addition to their political and social powers, the Atlanta papers were the font of all knowledge. If the phone rang on Saturday evenings, it often was someone who had had too much to drink and wanted the paper to settle an argument. When I received one of these calls, I envisioned a couple of guys sitting in a bar, drifting into an argument, the argument getting louder and more contentious, until one of them slammed his hand on the bar and said, "You want to bet on that? Let's call the paper." I helped solve many problems of the universe on Saturday evenings.

About 6:00 p.m. on this Saturday evening in February 1965, the phone rang. I picked it up, said, "City room"—God, I loved saying those words—and on the other end was a drunk asking if the Chattahoochee River merged with the Flint River in Georgia or Florida.

"Georgia," I told him.

He mumbled thanks, and before he hung up, I heard his triumphant shout to his friend, "You dumb shit. I told you it was Georgia."

The assistant city editor looked at me and grinned. "Off to an early start, are they?"

A few minutes later, the phone rang again. This time the city editor picked it up. He listened, turned to me with raised eyebrows, and repeated what the caller had told him: "Your friend called here and was told the two rivers merge in Georgia, and you don't believe it?"

I waved and sent frantic arm signals to the city editor. I mouthed, "Tell him Florida."

The city editor smiled and said, "I don't know who your friend talked to, but I am the editor here tonight, and I will tell you those rivers merge in Florida." He paused. "Everyone knows that."

Across the desk, I heard a triumphant, "I knew it," from the phone. Followed by "You lying son of a bitch, give me back my money."

Where that discussion went afterward, I do not know.

The editor and I were eating dinner at our desks, chatting in a desultory fashion, when the phone rang again. The editor shifted a bite around in his mouth, swallowed, and said, "City editor." He tensed, turned and pointed his finger at me, nodded several times, said, "We are on the way." Still holding the phone, he said, "Fire on the ground floor of the Hurt Building. Go."

The Hurt Building was an eighteen-story office building in the heart of downtown Atlanta.

The editor and I stared at each other for a frozen moment, both of us thinking the same thing: *Winecoff Hotel*. On December 7, 1946, the Winecoff, a hotel in downtown Atlanta, burned. It was the deadliest hotel fire in American history: 119 people died. A photographer won a Pulitzer for his picture of a woman caught in midfall after she jumped from an upper floor. And now, the horror of that night was the first thing that came to mind when we heard there was a fire in downtown Atlanta.

The editor clicked the phone to get a new line, turned to me, and said, "I'm calling the pressroom to tell them to get ready for a replate." His eyes widened. "Why are you still here?"

I grabbed my coat, stuck a notebook in my pocket, and walked toward the elevator. The Hurt Building was about five blocks away, but this was Saturday night and downtown Atlanta was wall-to-wall with thousands of people from the suburbs who came downtown to eat, see a movie, or saunter down the streets looking into store windows.

Five Points and Peachtree Street would be jammed, so I walked three blocks up Forsyth Street and cut across to Peachtree. The crowd watching the fire was about ten deep, filled the sidewalks and spilled onto Peachtree.

I pushed through saying, *"Atlanta Journal. Atlanta Journal."* People turned and looked at me in annoyance. But they stepped aside. Everyone stepped aside for the Atlanta papers.

At the edge of the crowd, I was on Peachtree Street, which was jammed with fire trucks, fire hoses, and police cars. Policemen were trying to push the crowd back to the sidewalk across the street from the fire.

The Hurt Building was a triangular-shaped building. Commercial spaces on the ground floor had plate-glass windows. Through those windows, I saw demonic orange flames dancing in roiling black smoke. Sirens wailed. Police officers on the curb faced the crowd but kept glancing over their shoulders and seeing the fire spreading to other stores.

I stepped out farther in the street, waved my notebook at a police officer, said, *"Atlanta Journal."*

"Be my guest," the officer said. And from his tone, it was clear he believed newspaper reporters were insane. "Stay behind the firemen. Don't get any closer."

I stood in the middle of Peachtree Street, studying the fire, watching the police and firemen, and glancing back at the Saturday night crowd. Taking notes. The sidewalk was packed for a block in both directions. They were getting the excitement they came to see, and their eyes were bright in light from the fire. Now black smoke was boiling and tumbling behind the plate-glass windows as if looking for an escape route. Jets of fire squirted through the smoke.

Suddenly, the front of the building exploded, and a sheet of fire and glass shards blasted across Peachtree Street. The heavy boom of the explosion echoed and rolled along the canyon of high-rise buildings. I managed a half turn away before the explosion pushed fire and glass at me and knocked me to my knees, dazed.

The crowd panicked. Dozens of people sprawled on Peachtree Street, many screaming, all frightened. Those still on the sidewalk had turned into a mob, everyone scrambling to get away, to get back to the suburbs.

My hands were shaking as I picked up my notebook and resumed taking notes. A flashbulb exploded in front of me, and I saw one of our photographers, backing off, looking at me with an expression of disbelief. I heard more sirens and knew ambulances from Grady Hospital, about ten blocks away, were racing to the fire. EMTs jumped out and walked among people on the street, loading some on stretchers and into ambulances. The clothing of many spectators was red with blood. There were not enough ambulances, and police were loading people into police cars and hauling them to Grady.

I was on my feet, shaky, still taking notes, when someone grabbed my shoulder and spun me around. It was Orville Gaines, who had been the paper's police reporter for as long as anyone could remember. He was more cop than reporter.

"You're going to Grady," he said, motioning toward a nearby police officer. He shouted to the officer.

"He okay?" the cop said.

By now, Orville had his arm around my waist and was half carrying me. "Some glass cuts. But I don't think anything serious." He looked at me. "Maybe in shock." He jiggled me a bit to see if I was coherent and said, "Well, young reporter, next time you cover a fire, you will remember what firemen call back pressure. Smoke built up inside and exploded."

I mumbled that I had to write a story. Orville said another *Journal* reporter happened to be downtown and would write the story. I had to go to the hospital. Maybe I could write a first-person sidebar about being caught in the explosion. If I was able.

At Grady, Orville, still half carrying me, forced his way to the front of a long row of bleeding people, some standing, some on gurneys, all with horror and panic on their faces. Blood splotches spread across the floor. The police officer cleared the way for us.

At the head of the line, Orville grabbed a doctor's arm and said, "Fix him up. Now. He's on deadline." Everyone in the ER knew Orville and rushed to do his bidding.

I took off my coat. It was shredded. I took off my bloody shirt. "Look at his hair," Orville said, half in curiosity, half in amazement. "And his eyebrows."

He leaned closer. "Damn, Coram. Your eyebrows are all gone, and your hair looks like somebody took a blowtorch to it."

He turned back to the doctor. "He hurt bad?"

"Drop your pants," the doctor ordered. I did, and the doctor looked me up and down, then spun me around.

"A dozen or so glass cuts. Lots of blood. Nothing serious."

Orville looked at his watch and instructed the doctor to put some alcohol on me and tape me up. He turned to a nearby police officer and asked if he would take me to the paper, about ten blocks west. "He's got to write this story. He's on deadline."

The officer nodded. I was amazed at how cops followed Orville's orders. I reached for my shirt. Orville laughed and said my shirt and jacket were ruined. But I should get dressed and get out. He said that in a half hour, he would call the other reporter with an update on the number of people injured. He would coordinate the coverage with the city editor. Ten minutes later, I was in the city room. The editor looked at my shredded coat and bloody shirt and said, "Orville called. You okay?"

"I'm okay."

"Orville said there are dozens of injured, a lot of them serious. The fire is not yet under control. Photo says they got good art." He named the other reporter whom he said would do the hard story. He paused. "You in shape to write a first-person sidebar about being caught in the explosion?" He paused again. "Orville said you were right in front of the building when it exploded, up there with the firemen."

I nodded.

"You know how lucky you are? Some of those people have serious injuries."

"I think so."

"I called your wife. I told her what happened but told her you were okay."

I winced. I had not thought of calling home.

The editor waved me away. "Get on it."

The next morning, stiff and sore, I limped to the front door, opened it, and picked up the Sunday paper. I took the paper out of the plastic bag, unfolded it, and stared at the front page a full thirty seconds.

A two-column story on the right side of the front page, above the fold, was my account of being in the middle of the explosion. Topping the story was a picture of me looking more than a little befuddled.

I had a byline and my picture on the front page of the Sunday paper. I shook my head and thought nothing could be better.

But it could, and it was. On Monday morning, when John Pennington came down the long hall toward the city room, he shouted in a voice heard throughout the sports department, the women's department, and across the city room. "Great job, Robert. Great job. You okay?"

Behind him sulked one of the other young reporters hired about the same time I had been hired. He was still doing rewrites and obits. He looked at me and shook his head. He stopped in front of my desk and looked me over. My eyebrows were gone. My hair scorched and curled. Bandages on my face. "You lucky son of a bitch."

Late that afternoon, I limped into my journalism class at Georgia State. My classmates looked at me and wondered if they really wanted to go into journalism. One student, a friend, leaned over and said, "Robert, you need to get a haircut. That look is not good."

The professor, who had spent twenty years in radio and had nothing but disdain for newspaper reporters, stood in front of the class, rocked on his heels, nodded my way, and said, "Mr. Coram, against my better judgment, I must congratulate you. A fine job of reporting spot news."

I wondered why I was still going to night school when I was doing the job I wanted to do.

22

I don't know where Bill Fields had his office, but it must have been in a deep freezer in the basement. Bill Fields was the executive editor, the unifying link between the news departments of both papers. He was a slight man of medium height, receding hairline, and stony visage. When he walked into the newsroom, eyes hooded, black-framed glasses held in his hand, his coat buttoned, and his face unsmiling, the temperature dropped twenty degrees.

No one in the newsroom had ever seen him laugh. But there were older reporters on the paper who said they had seen him smile. They could not remember the occasion.

From Bill Fields, I learned what it meant to be a loyal employee, a man who may have calumny and animosity heaped upon him, but who bears his burden with grace and who soldiers on. It was decades after he died that I learned his true story.

The mid-1960s were the height of the civil rights movement across the South. And the South did not always respond well. Georgia, Alabama, and Mississippi were known for their virulent opposition to change. Freedom Riders were beaten, and their buses were burned. Civil rights workers were being killed across the South, and all too often attempts to catch the perpetrators were less than enthusiastic.

Atlanta was the heart of the civil rights movement because Dr. Martin Luther King Jr. lived here. Daddy King, Andrew Young, Hosea Williams, and others lived here. Even so, there were many civil rights stories, both in Atlanta and around the South, that the Atlanta papers should have covered but didn't. A reporter might suggest a story and an editor might approve, but then a few hours later, the sheepish editor would tell the reporter to find something else to work on. We knew Bill Fields had killed the coverage. He was a seg. When racial subjects came up, he chewed on the rim of his glasses, looked at the ceiling, and walked away.

Then President Lyndon Johnson signed the Civil Rights Act of 1964, part of which was the public accommodations act. This act outlawed discrimination based on race, color, religion, or national origin.

The concept of private property is sacred in the South. Many people believed that a man's property is his to do with as he sees fit. That belief was best personified by the Atlanta man who owned the Heart of Atlanta Motel on Peachtree Street in midtown. He said the federal government did not have the right to tell him who he could admit or not admit to his restaurant. Bill Fields agreed with his logic because the motel owner got lots of coverage in the papers. The senior reporters who covered civil rights stories griped about having to give the motel owner such extensive coverage. They griped even more about how their stories were edited to make this seg look like he was saving the US Constitution from being ravaged. At the same time, we were giving this seg so much coverage we were not covering civil rights events that the wire services and national newspapers were covering.

Then came the day the public accommodations act was to go into effect, and Bill Fields knew he could not hold back the tide. On the day the act went into effect, my job was to start at Tenth Street in midtown and go out Peachtree Street as far as Piedmont Hospital and go inside every restaurant along the way, talk to restaurant managers, and see how they were reacting to the new law.

I asked John why was I starting in midtown, and he said we had to start north of the Heart of Atlanta Motel. He shrugged and said that since the owner of that motel was in litigation with the US government, we should not get involved. He looked at me, and I knew Fields had sent down the word.

When I went into restaurants and identified myself to the managers, they reacted as if I had the plague. It was with resignation and little enthusiasm they said they would follow the law.

I thought Atlanta was acquitting itself rather well. And then I walked into the restaurant at the Riviera Motel, located on Peachtree at the Downtown Connector. The front of the 250-room Riviera was parallel to Peachtree Street. The motel restaurant was one of the most popular in Atlanta, in part because the rear wall was glass and offered a view of the swimming pool.

But on this day the restaurant was closed. The maître d' hotel stood at the door, looking around as if afraid he was about to be invaded. I had a lot of ground to cover before my deadline and had no time for niceties. I walked up to the maître d', waved my notebook, and said, "*Atlanta Journal.* I need to ask you about the new law that goes into effect today and your policy toward black diners."

The middle-aged maître d' wore a dark suit and held a half-dozen menus cradled in his arm. His mouth opened and closed, but no sound came out.

"Why is your restaurant closed today, and what is your policy toward black diners? If they come in, will they be seated?"

He shuffled the menus, looked into the distance and said, "You will have to speak to the manager. I am not authorized to speak on that subject."

"Who told you to close the restaurant?"

"Who are you with again?"

"The *Atlanta Journal*."

A young black busboy standing against the wall turned his head toward me.

When the maître d' did not speak, I said, "Okay, who do I talk to? Where is the manager?"

"I am not sure. I don't believe he is on the property."

He walked away.

I could not find a supervisor in the restaurant, the halls, the kitchen, anywhere. The employees who were present were low-ranking and seemed to be mute. They leaned against the wall, fear in their eyes.

I still had numerous restaurants to visit and was about to leave when the young black busboy brushed passed me. His lips never moved when he whispered, "Office in the basement."

I grunted acknowledgment and realized once again that while there are people flushing pills down the toilet, there are also people who want to do the right thing, who will risk their jobs to see lawbreakers exposed. Reporters of that time would not have had much to write about had there not been so many Southerners, both black and white, of good will. These people were always there, and they stood up when they were needed.

I found the door to the basement, walked down the steep stairs, and opened another door onto a long dim hallway. One door was open, and light and voices spilled into the hall.

When I stepped into the open door, it took a moment for the three people inside to realize I was there. Large, muscular men stood on each side of a desk. The man sitting down was dressed in a gray silk suit, had hard eyes, slicked-back hair, and an imperious manner. He was handsome in a pimpish sort of way. "Who the hell are you?" he snapped.

"Robert Coram with the *Atlanta Journal*."

I was letting him know that no matter where they hid, no matter if they were owners, no matter what cards they held, being a newspaper reporter trumped them all. If I had told these men I was the Lord God Jehovah, I couldn't have gotten their attention any better.

"You gentlemen hiding down here?"

Mr. Slick Head almost exploded. "No, dammit, I am not hiding. This is a private office. And I could have you thrown out for trespassing."

"On the day the public accommodations law goes into effect, you want to charge a newspaper reporter with trespassing?"

He pursed his lips but said nothing. His two goons were leaning forward like chained Rottweilers awaiting the command.

The man behind the desk spoke in a soft voice when he asked me if I knew what would happen if he announced the Riviera welcomed black diners.

"You will be recognized as a businessman following the law."

"Smart ass," growled one of the goons.

Mr. Slick Head stood up and pointed toward the door, showing me his Big Boss demeanor. His two goons snarled. I don't think their regular jobs were in the restaurant business. These guys were not Southerners, nor was Mr. Slick Head. Their speech and manner had a hard edge; their dress was from Little Italy, and they were devoid of even a trace of courtesy.

"Not today," I said. This was a chance for me to go romping and stomping among bad guys, as invincible as if I had been wearing a suit of armor.

"Your dining room is closed," I added. "Is that an effort to keep black people out of the restaurant?"

One of the goons took a half step and in a deep mutter of a voice said, "I will tear you apart."

"That will make a front-page story."

Mr. Slick Head walked from behind his desk and pushed the muscle man aside. "Okay, reporter. We are closed a few days for repairs. We don't keep anybody out of our restaurant. We are open to all people." He held up a finger. "Just because you don't see a Frenchman or a person from China or a person from India sitting in my restaurant doesn't mean they are not welcome. All it means is they are not in the restaurant."

He smirked, and I knew he was thinking, "Top *that*, reporter boy."

I did a quick draw with my notebook, opened it, poised my pen over it, and said, "So I can quote you as saying black people are welcome in your restaurant?"

"No, don't write that shit down. I won't have any customers if you say black people are welcome." He paused, then threw his hands wide. "Hey, this is off the record, but—"

"I don't do off the record."

Both goons growled, and their boss waved them back and for a long moment did not speak. "Look, if I say black people are welcome, I will lose every white customer I have. If I say they are not welcome, FBI agents will be knocking on my door an hour after your paper hits the street. The Department of Justice is waiting for someone in the South to defy the new law." He looked at me, expecting sympathy. I stared. He resumed talking. "You can quote me as saying this restaurant will follow the law . . . disirregardlessly of a customer's race, creed, or . . ." He dribbled off and turned to one of his goons, held out a hand palm up as if saying, "Help me out here."

The goon shrugged, contorted his face and said, "We know the law. We will obey the law."

He had some difficulty with the second sentence.

I was having trouble with *disirregardlessly*, a word I did not think I would find in my dictionary.

"So, I can say that when your restaurant reopens . . . when will that be, by the way?"

"Tomorrow."

"Okay, I can say that tomorrow your restaurant will be open to all people?"

"You can say we will follow the law and welcome anyone who walks in the door." He grimaced. "Okay. Okay. You got what you wanted. Now get the hell out of here. I have a business to run."

"Thank you for your help," I said.

"Yeah, yeah." He waved me away.

God, but I loved riding my white horse.

THE South was evolving. It was a slow and often reluctant evolution, and it was clear to us reporters that Bill Fields did not like evolution. And we did not like the play the restaurant integration stories were getting in the *Journal*. Too often, they were below the fold. And the follow-up stories were always inside. But Fields had considerable power over coverage of stories and the placement of those stories.

By 1965, demonstrations were flaring up in towns across the South. Alabama seemed to have more than its share of both demonstrators and violent reaction by local and state law enforcement. In mid-February, a protester in Alabama was shot by a state trooper. Black people by the hundreds poured into Alabama, determined to break the back of segregation.

Selma had become the flashpoint of the civil rights movement.

This was the biggest story in the country. Reporters from the wire services and every major newspaper in America converged on Selma. But there was no reporter from the Atlanta papers. We seethed in anger and embarrassment. We knew Fields was the reason.

A reporter named Paul Valentine sat at the desk adjacent to mine. Paul was a slender man whose refined and intellectual appearance masked a passionate newsman. He was outspoken in his indignation that the *Journal* was not covering the civil rights movement as well as he thought it should be covered. Almost never did we send a reporter out of town to cover sit-ins or marches or demonstrations. And Dr. Martin Luther King Jr. did not receive the coverage in the *Journal* that he did in other papers around the country.

Now the civil rights story was reaching a bloody climax in Selma, and no one from the paper was there. A half dozen of us had begged John to send someone. John was embarrassed when he had to say, "Mr. Fields said we didn't need to send anyone, that we could use wire copy." Paul and I agreed we would confront Mr. Fields.

One morning in early February, Paul saw Fields coming down the hall. He leaned toward me and said, "Let's go."

We stood up. Paul went to the right of his desk, and I went to the left of mine, causing us to converge on Fields from different angles.

"Mr. Fields," I said.

He stopped, stared, and did not speak.

"Could we talk?"

"Who is we?"

I pointed to Paul on the other side of Mr. Fields and said, "Paul and me."

The newsroom was a frozen tableau. Editors and reporters alike stared at us, knowing what we were doing. Bill Fields turned his icy stare at Paul and said, "What is it?"

"Mr. Fields, we want to talk with you about sending a reporter to Selma," Paul said in his earnest tone. "National papers, network TV people, even a lot of weeklies around the South are covering that story. We think the *Journal* should be there."

Fields nibbled on the frame of his glasses. "You do?" His voice was filled with sarcasm.

Paul did not waver. "Yes, sir, I do. Our masthead says we cover Dixie like the dew. And we are not covering a national event about a hundred miles away in Alabama."

"I suppose you want me to send you two?"

Paul doubled down. "No, sir. We are not asking you to send us. We are asking that you send somebody, anybody." He waved his hand across the newsroom. "This is the biggest ongoing story in the country, and we should be there."

"You two trying to make a name for yourselves? Is that what you want?" Fields darted his eyes between Paul and me.

"Mr. Fields," I said, "Every reporter on the paper would love to go. But who you send doesn't matter. What matters is that the paper should be there."

Fields snorted. "You think that is a reason you should be there." He looked at me with disgust. At that moment, I knew I had been put into the troublemaker category.

"The wire services are doing a good job," Fields said. "Haven't you seen those stories?"

"Yes, sir," Paul said. "But the point is this newspaper should have a dateline out of Selma. We should not rely on the wires."

"They are marching over the Edmund Pettus Bridge tomorrow," Paul said. "People are going to get hurt. It will be violent. King and Young are leaders of the march, and they are from Atlanta."

Fields had enough. He chewed on the frame of his glasses, eyes darting from Paul to me and back to Paul. The three of us sensed that work on the city desk, the news desk, the photo desk, and the copy desk had stopped. Everyone was staring.

Fields spoke. In a voice heard all over the newsroom, he said, "We will send someone to Selma when the situation justifies it."

He turned and walked out of the newsroom.

"Racist son of a bitch," Paul whispered.

At that moment, I realized that the soul of a newspaper, its moral force, comes not because it simply is a newspaper but because its voice is a trumpet blasting into a dark world, its pages a bright light that illuminates every corner. Newspapers are revered because they are *for* something that is good and noble and right. They represent ideas that history will validate. They represent standards that will be remembered. They lay the foundation for history.

PAUL took a few days' vacation. When he returned, he announced that he had been hired by the *Washington Post*. There, he would have a long and distinguished career. Another civil rights reporter, Walter Rugaber, left to work for the *New York Times*.

It would be years before I discovered how wrong we all were about Bill Fields. He was a good newspaperman with good instincts. It was the top management of the papers, a taciturn and rotund fellow we called "Big Thunder," who wanted to limit civil rights coverage. And he wanted to limit the coverage because the paper's defamation lawyers insisted he do so. The paper was facing a $10 million suit over McGill's columns. The Atlanta papers were the cash cow for the Cox chain, which owned the papers, and the papers did not want to be on the wrong end of a defamation suit. Lawyers wanted to take the safe road and said additional inflammatory civil rights stories could harm their defense of the paper.

Bill Fields was a good newspaperman and was a good soldier. He accepted the calumny and disdain of reporters because he was doing what his boss told him to do.

I have often wondered how Bill Fields felt inside about all this, about how he kept these things bottled up in his heart. I wish I had known at the time. I wish we had all known. We would have been much more comfortable criticizing lawyers than we were criticizing Bill Fields. In the end, Fields took a hit for the lawyers. And that is a fate that should not be wished on anyone.

In the fullness of time, the suit against the papers was thrown out of court.

But it would be forever remembered that the Atlanta papers were not at Selma.

23

Working at the paper changed me in a profound way. I found that every waking hour was oriented toward the paper. No matter what happened, no matter who told me something in confidence, my first thought was, "How can I get that in the paper?" Everything I heard or read, I thought of as a possible newspaper story. Such an attitude is off-putting to one's friends and scary to one's family.

Leslie realized just how much I had changed not long after she took a job as assistant to the manager of a radio station. The manager was also head of the Republican Party in Georgia. Leslie often typed letters from him to party executives. The letters often were of the cheerleading variety because the Republicans were having a tough go of it in the land of Yellow Dog Democrats.

One night at dinner, Leslie told me about a letter she had typed for her boss. I don't recall the specifics, but I do recall that the letter contained tactics the Republicans would use in the next election. I knew the letter would make a good story. I wrote the story. It was on the front page.

I don't know who was more surprised to see the story in the paper: Leslie or her boss. Like most cheerleaders, her boss was a smiling and jovial fellow. But the day my story came out, he struggled to control his anger. He told Leslie he would fire her but that if he did, the *Journal* would get all huffy and write a follow-up story about what a mean Republican he was. And then there would be a critical editorial about the Republican Party. He was not going to fire her. But if he ever again saw the contents of one of his letters in the newspaper again, she would be looking for a new job.

That evening at dinner was the first time I ever saw Leslie angry. She raised her voice when she asked why I had written the story. And she was dumbstruck when I said I wrote it because I thought it was a good story, a judgment call verified by the fact it was on the front page.

"But I was talking to you as my husband, not as a newspaper reporter."

"You didn't tell me it was off the record."

She stared in disbelief. "Why should I preface our conversations by saying something is off the record?"

"Because if you don't, I assume it is on the record."

"Every conversation?"

"If there is a story in it, yes."

She stared, tried to say something, but then shook her head, stood up, and walked away.

At that moment, something happened between us. It was as if we were standing on opposite sides of a river speaking different languages. We realized that newspapering was the consuming interest in my life, that a story took precedence over everything.

That awareness frightened both of us.

WHAT was once called a newspaper reporter is today called a "content provider." For old reporters, a content provider is just another Joe Shit the Ragpicker. There is not a whiff of the romantic or the crusader or the righter of wrongs about him. Rather, there is the odious stench of a person who has debased a once-noble craft. He is a plowman whose professional antecedents rode white horses.

At the *Journal*, we had two expressions about our profession. The first was "We comfort the afflicted, and we afflict the comfortable." The second was "We start fires, or we put out fires."

Yes, there is more than a little of the self-righteous in such expressions. But that is what we believed. That is what we lived.

By 1966, John Pennington had become a columnist, and I became the *Journal*'s primary investigative reporter. I was as aggressive as any reporter could be, almost certainly because I was afraid that I had overlooked something, that somewhere was someone who could add an electric surge to the story. There was always one more person to interview. Always. Because of my aggressiveness, I was threatened with physical violence and was told, "I will own your newspaper," but it signified nothing. I was never sued.

I would have spent my career at the *Journal*. But the demon that had slept for more than past five years awakened. I was off on was another Quixotic rampage, not unlike when I was a draftsman working with atomic bombs and left my desk to get drunk; not unlike a promising job at Milledgeville where I helped a patient escape; not unlike being fired from my first three jobs in Atlanta.

For reasons I did not understand then and do not understand now, I took the lead in an effort to organize *Journal* reporters into a labor union. Even today, I don't know why I did this. I don't like labor unions. Working conditions at the paper were good. And I knew from the beginning that reporters would not vote for the union. I was right. The outcome of the election was not even close. The union failed by an embarrassing vote count. Now I was a dead man walking. In order to send a message that union efforts would not be tolerated, management would have to fire me. The showdown came six months later over a story I did about Atlanta night clubs and Georgia's blue laws.

A particular bar whose owner had been outspoken in fighting the blue laws was raided and shut down. Clubs whose owners had remained quiet stayed open.

Anyone with common sense knew the state's action was punitive. But no one would say so. I called the state revenue commissioner whose office enforced the blue laws and told him a senior police officer told me the raid was punitive. The angry revenue commissioner said, "He should not have told you that. We agreed not to go public on this manner." Now the commissioner had confirmed the raid was punitive.

I had not talked to a police officer. The only confirmation I had about the raid was from the revenue commissioner. He had fallen for the oldest trick in the book: when no one will talk about something you know to be true, tell them you already know. Every time they will give you a quote saying it is true.

The revenue commissioner was furious. He called the paper and said I had tricked him, that what I had done was unethical. The governor joined in and said I was unethical and would no longer be allowed in his office.

Now the paper had the reason it had waited for. On August 11, 1967, Fields called me to his office. A half-dozen subeditors were there to act as witnesses. They were solemn-faced and found their shoes of extraordinary interest. Fields fired me, saying I had violated the canon of journalistic ethics by deceiving a source in order to get material for a story.

The experience was more painful than I can ever express, not so much for being fired as for being accused of ethical faults in a job that I loved.

Few things in life are as painful as being fired from the job you thought you would hold until you were old and dotty. For about six months, I wallowed in pain such as I had never before known. All of my past failures mixed together did not hurt as much as being fired from the newspaper.

Other reporters had misrepresented themselves in order to get a story. John Pennington had grown a beard, rented a car with New Jersey plates, and gone to McIntosh County posing as a Yankee tourist. When the city editor received a letter saying the director of a halfway house was incompetent in dealing with mental patients just released from Milledgeville, he passed the letter to me and said follow up on this. He thought it funny when I called the director and passed myself off as a mental patient who had just been released from the state hospital. It was easy. I remembered how Billy had behaved.

The medical examiner of Fulton County once reacted to a story I wrote by saying he would never talk to me again. When I needed material for a story I was writing about a murder, I called the medical examiner's office and identified myself as another *Journal* reporter. The city editor thought this was clever.

When the data processing chief of Fulton County would not give me a voter-profile study, I told him his superior had approved the release of the study. He then gave me the study. The city editor thought this displayed initiative.

A *Constitution* reporter was researching an article about brutality, poor food, drug traffic, and horrific conditions in the Atlanta penal system. He let his hair grow long, poured whiskey over his clothes, and insulted an Atlanta police officer, all for the purpose of being arrested and confined to the city prison farm.

Reuben Smith, from the courthouse beat, pretended to be a lawyer in order to obtain a court record involving the state purchasing agent who had been accused of usury.

The list of what I saw as comparable but unpunished incidents was endless. But it was to no avail. I was fired.

DURING my years at the paper, if someone had asked, "Who are you?" I would have said I am a newspaper reporter. I would have made the terrible mistake of defining myself by my work. Now, when I lost my job, I was nothing.

The pain was amplified in the coming months when I met reporters or politicians on the street or at the grocery store, and they snubbed me.

Elected officials who had kissed my ass when I was at the paper, people who had invited me to dinner in their homes, now would barely nod when we met. I had assumed that these people liked me because they thought I was a great guy. Now I realized it was the reporter they were inviting and not me.

I wandered through a desert of burning pain and swore that I would never again identify myself by my work. My work was what I did. But it was not who I was. If I ever were fired again, I would not stumble. I would be at full power the next day.

The good news, which I did not recognize for years, was that I had been fired when I was young and resilient. And while being fired pained me, I was not incapacitated as were those who hold a job for twenty years and then are fired when they are in their fifties. At the time, few recovered. They knew there was no place for them to go, and that this was the end of their working life. They lived out long years of bitterness.

I had been unemployed for about six months when Reuben Smith called. He had left the paper to become bureau chief for *Business Week* magazine. Rube said that McGraw-Hill, which published *Business Week*, had a news bureau in Atlanta and the bureau needed a reporter. He had recommended me for the job.

I thought McGraw-Hill published books. I did not know they also published more than forty trade magazines. *Business Week* and *Aviation Week* were the magazines best known to the public. But the other magazines, while not widely known, had ecclesiastical weight within their respective industries.

Engineers and architects poured over *Engineering News-Record* as if it were the Bible.

Many McGraw-Hill magazines were controlled circulation. *Medical World News* was read by some 110,000 doctors across America and was the most influential medical magazine in the country.

I thought reporting for trade magazines was a backward step in my career. Reporting for a trade magazine was little more than compiling lists. It was formulaic collections of material. This was not a place to *write*, not a place to strut my stuff. But it was a job, and I had a wife. In the two-person McGraw-Hill bureau, I was number two.

In a short time, working for these prosaic trade magazines would take me on my first grand adventure as a writer, an adventure I would never have experienced at the newspaper, an adventure I would remember all my life. Halfway around the world, a big story awaited me.

It would be years before I realized this great adventure would never have happened had I not been fired.

24

Two years after I went to McGraw-Hill, Roland walked in. I don't remember his last name, probably because he was one of those louche, shifty-eyed outliers known to every reporter. These guys pop up from time to time, sometimes with a great story, always with an agenda. But, then, every source has an agenda.

Roland's agenda was respectability. He wanted respectability in his hometown of Nashville, Tennessee. He had raised money to donate to Biafra, a breakaway state waging civil war against Nigeria.

Biafra had seceded in May 1967, and a year later the overwhelming might of Nigeria had squeezed the breakaway state into a small and beleaguered place whose destiny was doom. Roland had been to Biafra three times. He said he went to look around and to write reports that he used to raise what he called "a lot of money" for Biafra. He said he knew the president of Biafra, General Chukwuemeka Odumegwu Ojukwu. Newspaper reporters in Nashville thought Roland was a fraud and wanted proof that the money he had raised went to Biafra. I could understand why Roland's hometown newspaper thought he was a fraud. He had greasy hair, his sideburns were too long, he had an ingratiating manner, and no apparent means of support. How could a man like this know the president of Biafra? Why would this nobody raise several hundred thousand dollars to give to Biafra? These questions could easily have been answered if a reporter had accompanied Roland to Biafra. But no Nashville reporters would go to Biafra to document the money trail.

Like so many people around the South, Roland came to Atlanta to find salvation. He wanted reporters to accompany him to Biafra. He would advise reporters on the byzantine procedure of getting into Biafra. And he would guarantee an interview with General Ojukwu.

Roland approached reporters at the Atlanta newspapers, *Atlanta Magazine*, and the bureau chiefs of national newspapers and magazines based in Atlanta. These writers called friends in Nashville, who said Roland was a fraud.

And that is how Roland wound up at the McGraw-Hill News Bureau. Except for people in the industries covered by McGraw-Hill magazines, few knew of the bureau. Nor did they care. Very little we published was ever seen by the public. To the public, to mainstream newspapers, and to regional and national magazines, we did not exist.

I was Roland's last hope. That explains why he was deferential, almost obsequious, when he came into my office. He was a wiry man dressed in cheap slacks, a cheap shirt, and cheap shoes. He was intense, even messianic, on the subject of Biafra. He appeared to know everything there was to know about Biafra and had a quick and confident answer to every question.

He knew the background of the war, the main players, and every development. He said General Ojukwu was a tall and robust man of great charm, a charismatic Sandhurst graduate. And, perhaps most important of all, he was of the Ibo tribe.

The Ibo tribe of eastern Nigeria was the most intellectual of all Nigerian tribes. They were a small tribe but controlled most civil service jobs and were more than a little snooty toward the Hausa and Fulani, two much larger and more powerful tribes.

Boiled down and simplified, a small number of smart-assed Ibos took on the government of oil-rich Nigeria.

General Ojukwu was at war not only with Nigeria but with many world powers. British colonial masters had carved out Nigeria and did not want to see their handiwork changed. Britain came to the aid of Nigeria with everything from Saladin armored cars to machine guns.

The Soviets supplied jet aircraft, tanks, artillery, and trawlers that patrolled offshore to identify relief flights inbound from Sao Tome. The Portuguese possession of Sao Tome and Principe—islands forming a scruffy little fourth-world country—was home base for relief flights and weapons flights entering Biafra.

Except for selling Biafra a few tired cargo aircraft, America remained aloof from the war.

Once Biafra was encircled and closed off from the world, Biafrans began starving by the thousands. Then by the hundreds of thousands. Nigeria considered starvation to be a legitimate weapon of war. The only way to bring in food was by air. But to a small country engaged in a civil war, weapons were more important than food.

McGraw-Hill had no magazines that would be interested in a conventional story about the war. We would leave that to the mainstream media. But McGraw-Hill published two of the most respected medical magazines in America. And no reporter covering the Biafra war had dived into the medical aspects—the full measure of the starvation, diseases, lack of supplies, caliber of hospitals and medical care.

Roland said he could arrange for me to interview General Ojukwu and senior doctors. He could get me access to the biggest hospital in the country. My expression of doubt caused Roland to lean forward, look around as if afraid someone might hear him, and said, "Look, I *know* the general. I'm taking him a bag of money. He will do just about anything I want."

I sat back, thinking. Roland leaned ever closer and said, "But I want something in return." I stared, waiting. Almost like a little boy begging a favor, Roland said, "I want you to mention me somewhere in your story. And I want you to report that I brought money to General Ojukwu."

I could live with the tradeoff. But I would be writing medical stories, and I could not guarantee a mention in my stories. If Roland fitted into the story, I would include him. But no guarantees.

He nodded in understanding. This was one desperate man. He was depending on me, who was writing for a magazine unknown to the general public, to make him legitimate in Nashville.

My boss, the bureau chief, was a very proper, reserved, and elegant middle-aged woman with white hair and an air of equanimity. I wish I could remember her name. I do remember that when I told her I wanted to go to Africa, she pursed her lips, tapped her pencil on her desk, got herself under control, and in a clipped voice said, "Robert, this is the *Atlanta* news bureau. We cover the southeast. Not Africa."

Good point. But every young writer needs a war, and this was my war. I agreed with her but added that this could be a big story for *Medical World News*, one of our most prestigious magazines and one we rarely wrote for.

She tapped her pencil on her desk and stared at me, impassive.

"It would also increase the standing of the Atlanta bureau."

She turned her chair ninety degrees to look at the wall. She waited a long moment. With great reluctance, she said, "Do you think you can get commitments out of enough magazines to finance the trip?"

This was the key question. When we traveled, which was not often, it was always on assignment for a magazine, and expenses were charged to that magazine. But this trip would cost a great deal and would have to be approved in advance by New York.

"Yes, ma'am. I do."

"You do that, and I am sure New York will approve the trip."

She was not happy about my being away for an unknown length of time. She would have to do my job as well as her own job. But this was initiative that would make her look good at the home office. The Atlanta bureau had the inside track on a story that New York had not considered.

Leslie could not understand my running off to Africa to cover a war. We had Kimberly, our new six-month-old daughter, and Leslie did not want to become a single parent for several weeks, maybe a month.

"It's my job," was all I could say. I was determined to make the trip. I needed a war. And this one was in Africa, the Dark Continent, far off and mysterious Africa. This was my big chance, and I would do whatever it took to be there.

My timing could not have been better. Fiery young civil rights activists were going to Africa to encourage the revolution. A few publications were beginning to write David-versus-Goliath stories. But no one had published a medical story about the war.

Editors at *Medical World News* were easy to convince. They were stereotypical New Yorkers in that they thought the South was a dark and cruel and weird racist swamp but that the gods, with a twisted cosmic humor, blessed Southern writers with something special. I had met a number of McGraw-Hill editors. When they looked at me, I felt as if I were Turkana Boy being examined by Richard Leakey. The editors smirked at my accent and laughed at my white socks, but they liked my work. And once I told them I had lined up an interview with General Ojukwu who, in turn, would approve my visiting the largest medical facilities in the country and interviewing the top doctors, it was easy. Not only did they agree to finance the trip, but also they volunteered to bring in another hospital magazine published by McGraw-Hill. This spread out the expenses and made the trip more palatable to the accountants.

Now I would be writing a story that would go in two magazines and on a topic McGraw-Hill had not covered.

The editors at *Medical World News* asked me to spend one day at their offices before leaving for Africa. As is the way of editors, they wanted to feel they were the architects of the story. They wanted to tell me what questions to ask.

Roland briefed me on the logistics of the trip. Every Monday night at midnight, a relief flight bound for Sao Tome took off from Schiphol airport in Amsterdam. Roland said if I could get to Amsterdam, he would arrange for me to fly on the cargo flight at no expense. This was a big selling point for my story.

I planned to spend Monday in New York and fly to Amsterdam on the overnight flight. That meant I missed the weekly flight to Sao Tome and would wait in Amsterdam until the next flight. A week on an expense account. Carpe per diem, I always say. I talked to everyone I could find who had been to Amsterdam, and they agreed that the Grand Hotel Krasnapolsky was the place to stay.

In January 1969, I kissed my daughter and my wife goodbye and left on the first leg of my trip. Leslie's last words to me were to make sure I visited the Rijksmuseum in Amsterdam. She saw my blank look and added, "It is a museum. One of the world's great museums. And be sure you see *The Night Watch*."

"*Night Watch*? Is that the security guards?" I asked.

She smiled. "Ask the museum staff. They will know."

In New York, I stayed at the Algonquin. When I walked through the lobby, I imagined Dorothy Parker, Robert Benchley, George S. Kaufman, Harold Ross, and the other members of what they called "The Vicious Circle," sitting at a round table dropping bon mots that would endure for years.

My meeting with editors at *Medical World News* made them feel they were a part of the story. I wrote down all their suggested questions and told them these were great questions that I would never have thought about. Now the editors were vested.

Toward midafternoon, I went to the Plaza Hotel to the Oak Room and had a Scotch. I had never drunk Scotch before, but it seemed the thing to do. Anthony Perkins, a star famous for his role in *Psycho*, was sitting at the next table. He kept his eyes on his plate, but I am sure he was aware of those of us looking at him.

And then I was off to cover a war.

25

JANUARY is not a big month for tourists in Amsterdam, and it seemed I had the city to myself. I walked snowy streets, gawked at ancient canals, and imagined myself as a cosmopolitan war correspondent. The Dam, the large plaza in front of the Krasnapolsky, was a gathering place for young people from all across Europe. They sat in the cold, smoked joints, and railed against "the Man."

I ate the famous Rijsttafel, the elaborate Indonesian meal adopted by the Dutch, and coasted through a very cold week. The trip to the Rijksmuseum began with a query to the phlegmatic desk clerk at the Krasnapolsky. He perked up and gave me precise instructions. He added that the museum was conducting maintenance. If I wanted to see *The Night Watch*, there would be no line.

I was thirty-three, yet all I knew about art was what I picked up from an art appreciation class at Georgia State. In southwest Georgia, there were no art galleries, no museums, no theaters, no lectures, no concerts. All we had was cotton and corn and peanuts and a way of life that lingered in the past. In Amsterdam, I was a tabula rasa and absorbing sights and sounds and smells and the feeling of the city.

At the Rijksmuseum, I wandered through empty rooms and down long halls. I passed bored security guards and found myself in a narrow lane formed by flimsy plastic sheets put up by maintenance workers. After moving through the semidarkness, I rounded a corner and found myself in a dim room facing a painting, the only painting in the room. A security guard stood in the corner. He gave me a quick look and settled back into a comfortable position, staring straight ahead and staying in his happy place.

The dim light of the museum melded with the darkness of the painting until the physical outlines of the painting were no more, and what I saw was a group of men seeming to march toward me. For the first time in my life, I was transfixed by the emotion that can sweep over a person in the presence of great art. I sucked in my breath. Tears came to my eyes. I swayed in the semidarkness and leaned to the right to get out of the way of the people in the painting. I did not know what I was looking at. I did not know about the subtleties of color in the painting. I did not know what the painting represented or the parts of the painting hidden in plain sight.

But what I did know was that I was in the presence of greatness. And I knew that Rembrandt had been touched by the hand of God.

When I left the museum, my thoughts tumbled. The day was gray and rainy and cold. But I hardly noticed. I could not escape the impact of the painting. I was uncomfortable with the feelings boiling inside me, feelings I had never known before.

I was the single passenger aboard the cargo flight to Sao Tome. The pilot of the DC-6 nodded, told me to sit anywhere I wanted. I had my choice of boxes or bags. Most of the cargo was hundred-pound bags of a powdered substance that, when mixed with water, formed a high-carbohydrate meal. The remainder of the cargo was medical supplies.

After takeoff, the pilot motioned me forward and pointed to the jump seat between him and the copilot. From Amsterdam to Paris is about 270 miles. A half hour after takeoff, I watched the lights of Paris pass under the wing. My God . . . Paris, the City of Light. After a while, I napped on a bag of powdered food, serene in the airplane smell of oil and hydraulic fluid and old leather.

I awakened when we landed in Tunisia to refuel. I looked out the window and saw a man clothed from head to boot in Arab garb, riding a camel, and motioning the pilot where he should park.

A man on a camel directing an aircraft to a refueling area. Only in Africa.

That afternoon we landed at Sao Tome, a bird-splatter of an island sitting almost atop the equator. As we completed the roll-out, the pilot and copilot opened the cockpit windows, and a blast of heat funneled into the aircraft. I smelled salt air and felt the tension and the urgency found at an airport where aircraft are departing for a war zone.

At ground level, all airports look alike: long runways, taxiways, mowed grass and some sort of terminal building. This one was different because of the type of aircraft that dominated the tarmac.

A dozen large multiengine cargo aircraft, most of them DC-6s and DC-7s, sat nearby, cargo doors open. Judging by the oil-streaked engines and weary sag of the aircraft, they had flown many miles. They were being loaded with food by low-key and smiling men.

A half mile away was another group of cargo aircraft. Men driving forklifts were loading heavy boxes. "What is that?" I asked the copilot.

"Guns and ammo," he said. The men loading these aircraft were intense men, moving with confidence, and surrounded by armed guards.

We inched to a stop, and when the wide cargo doors opened, Roland was the first person I saw. He was smiling. One hand was waving; the other was clutching a green gym bag. A few steps behind was a well-tailored man in a black suit. I wondered how the hell anyone could wear a suit in this heat. He must be a banker or a bureaucrat.

I picked up my small bag and climbed down the ladder. Roland and I shook hands, and then Roland said, "Give me your passport." He passed it to the man in the black suit, who walked ahead of us, thumbing through the passport. The man stopped, looked back at me, and gave the passport to an immigration official, who stamped it and returned it. The man in the black suit put the passport in his pocket.

"Hey, what about my passport?" I said.

He ignored me. He had a quick whispered conversation with Roland. Roland looked at him in surprise, nodded, and said, "Would you? Thanks."

Roland picked up my bag. "Let's have a drink, and I'll brief you," he said. He pointed to a cab with the back door open. "We need to talk. The bar is a half mile away."

"I'd like to have a shower and change clothes. Let's go to the hotel first."

Roland laughed and said there was but one hotel on Sao Tome, and it was filled with pilots and with journalists. The hotel was full and had a long waiting list. Roland said, "I got a reservation for you at a posada. It's a ten-minute cab ride. You can go there after we have a drink."

"What's a posada?"

"Room. Bath at the end of the hall. No meals. Don't worry. You're not going to be here long enough to even think about it." He laughed and slapped me on the back. I jumped. I don't like to be slapped on the back. "You are going into Africa, my friend," Roland said. "A different world."

Being alone and out in the country did not appeal to me. I told Roland that I appreciated all he had done, but I did not want to stay out in the boonies. I don't speak Portuguese. Where do I eat? I wiped dripping perspiration from my face and shrugged my shoulders, trying to unstick my shirt from my back. "And who the hell is that guy in the black suit, and why is he hanging around?"

Roland laughed and reached out to slap me on the back again. I moved away.

"You won't be there but one night," he said. "Bring your bag when you come in tomorrow morning. We'll have breakfast and hang around until we take off about dark." He laughed. "You are lucky I could get you a room in the posada. The international press has flooded this place. Somebody told them a war was on."

The man in the black suit moved to the front seat of the cab as Roland and I got into the back. "The bar is the coolest place around. There is no air conditioning in Sao Tome. But the bar has a patio that gets a good sea breeze."

I looked at Roland and bent my head toward the man in the black suit. "A friend," Roland whispered. "I'll explain later."

I scrambled for my notebook as he began talking, dumping information on me: late tomorrow afternoon, we'd take off and go to Uli Airport in Biafra. Relief pilots called the airport "Airstrip Annabelle." It was a widened strip of road, but it was the second busiest airport in Africa. Every hundred yards or so, fingers jutted off the runway to allow aircraft a place to pull off and unload. Slit trenches were along the runway. If bombs started falling, we were to jump into the nearest slit trench. More than fifty flights came every night. All flights came in after dark and left before sunrise. Every flight broke a half-dozen international laws. From dark to dawn, aircraft landed minutes apart. More than two hundred fifty tons of supplies every night. More than two dozen pilots had been killed. It was one of the greatest relief operations in history

I could not process so much information. My mouth was open. "Bombs start falling? Bombs? What the hell are you talking about? I work for trade publications. We don't do bombs."

Roland shrugged and said the Nigerians did not know which aircraft were carrying food and which aircraft were carrying arms and ammo. So they bombed the runway every time the landing lights came on. The lights wouldn't be turned on until our aircraft was maybe thirty seconds out, and sometimes that was enough time for a bomber to get lined up.

"Is there any other way to get into Biafra?"

Roland laughed.

By now we were at the hotel, a one-story building with a wing of maybe twenty rooms. The main part of the building opened onto a patio with several dozen small tables. Except for several waitresses, I saw no women. The khaki pants, boots, cotton shirts, and—most of all—their manner told me the customers were pilots or reporters. The manner of the pilots was subdued, and most of them were drinking nonalcoholic drinks. Their eyes kept roaming about, watching every person who entered and turning up toward the sky every time an aircraft flew over. The manner of the reporters was loud and laden with ego, and they were drinking beer. Lots of beer. Their mood was either ingratiating or arrogant; it depended on whether they were trying to wheedle something out of a pilot or if they were in their natural state.

A few feet behind the open bar was an ocean of astonishing blue. Not a cloud was in the sky. Heat waves shimmered from the ground. A cool breeze brought the smell of the sea mixed with tropical flowers. It was exotic and unique and laden with the air of danger.

The man in the black suit pointed to a corner table. Empty, and with an armed guard standing over it to make sure it remained empty. As Roland and I walked toward the table, the man in the black suit jumped back into the cab.

"Roland, what about my passport?" I said in confusion. Roland guided me through the crowd and toward the table. He held his gym bag in front. A few men around the tables nodded at him, their eyes cautious.

I pulled on Roland's arm and stopped him. "You got an armed guard holding a table for us? And where is my passport?"

"My friend who just left did that for me. There are Nigerian spies here, and I have to be careful." He looked around. "Oh, there you are," he said to the man behind us. A waiter.

As we sat down, I leaned across the table and said, "Why do you have to be careful, and who the hell is the guy in the black suit?"

Roland shifted his eyes from side to side, looking all around but not moving his head. He held the gym bag on his lap, pulled the zipper down a few inches, and spread the edges apart. The bag was jammed full of bank-wrapped packages of hundred-dollar bills. Roland put a long forefinger on one package and whispered, "Ten thousand dollars a bundle."

I leaned back and whispered, "Holy shit."

"This money is for General Ojukwu; the money I promised him; the money I want you to see me deliver." He looked around. "The guy in the black suit is a personal aide to General Ojukwu. His money man. The general assigned him and the fellow with the rifle to be with me until I get on the aircraft tomorrow."

He stared at me for a long moment, and in a slow and measured fashion, said, "You have no visa for Biafra. How do you expect to get into the country?"

In disbelief, I said, "Visa? I got a visa for Sao Tome. Biafra is not a country. Why would I need a visa?"

Roland leaned closer. "Little would-be countries like Biafra want to be thought of as legitimate in all aspects. One obvious way is to follow the rules of other countries and require visitors to have a visa. You should have gotten one in New York." He paused. "You will not get on that aircraft tomorrow without a visa."

I was panicked. Things were happening too fast. A few hours ago, I was flying over Paris. Then the guy on the camel directing the aircraft to a refueling pump. Now I was on a Portuguese island that, until a few weeks ago, I had never heard of, an island that required a diligent search on a detailed map to locate. I was in a bar overlooking the ocean and surrounded by mercenary pilots talking in a babel of languages. I was headed to an airport that was bombed every night. The guy across the table had several hundred thousand dollars in cash in a gym bag. And now my trip was compromised because I made the stupid mistake of not picking up a visa in New York. I would be fired if I came back with no story.

"What do you think that conversation at the airport was about?" Roland said. "You want a drink?"

I was in a stupor, watching my career go down the tubes. What sort of war correspondent was I if I assumed I would need no visa? I hate it when I do something that shows I am a bozo from southwest Georgia.

"You want a drink?" Roland repeated.

"Coke or lemonade. Extra ice."

Roland turned to the waiter, pointed at me, and said, "Coke for him. Beer for me."

He zipped the gym bag closed but kept it in his lap and with one hand curved through the handle.

"Roland, what am I going to do?"

He looked at me for a long moment and did not speak. He smiled a conspiratorial smile, leaned close, and said, "I can fix this."

26

Across the open courtyard, a cab stopped. The man in the black suit alighted, walked to Roland, and handed him my passport. Roland opened it, thumbed through, found what he was looking for, and turned it so I could see: a visa for Biafra.

"How . . . ?" I looked at the man in the black suit. He had backed a few steps away from the table. I was still angry at myself.

"How did you do this?" I demanded. "And so fast. Who are you?"

Roland's voice was calm. "I told you he is close to the president of Biafra. His personal representative here on Sao Tome. He has influence here."

I looked at the man in the black suit. He did not speak. Roland leaned across the table, smiled, waited a long moment and said, "What I did for you . . . the visa."

I tensed.

"Will cost you nothing. I arranged for your visa because I want you to document my giving this money to the president."

I nodded in silent thanks.

Roland raised his beer. "Drink up. Tomorrow we go to Africa."

Roland and I, along with two pilots, stood in front of a sagging DC-6. Streaks of oil stained the cowlings. I could see rust spots along the welds in the fuselage and wings. I shook my head. I'm going to Airstrip Annabelle in this tired old airplane. God only knows what the maintenance record is.

"What is our cargo?" I asked Roland.

"Ten tons of salt."

"Why salt?"

"Because people are dying of starvation. Whatever they find to eat, they need salt."

The man in the black suit stood a few feet away, not speaking, his eyes moving everywhere. Behind him stood the man from the restaurant, the one with the rifle. Roland and the pilots ignored them. But they made me nervous. Roland was holding onto his gym bag. He directed an airport worker to hoist my small shoulder bag, Roland's suitcase, and a box aboard the aircraft.

"Careful with that box," Roland said. "It is fragile." He turned to me, smiled, and said, "Case of Scotch."

"That salt tied down pretty well?" I asked the pilot. Just making conversation. And to show him I knew a bit about loading cargo aircraft.

He laughed. "Not tied down at all. When we land, we don't have time to untie cargo. It has to get out fast."

"What about turbulence?" I had visions of bags of salt flying around the interior of the aircraft.

"No weather. No turbulence. Annabelle is about four hundred miles from here. Flight is a little over two hours. It depends on if we are bombed on landing and have to circle, whether we have to make evasive maneuvers if we are shot at."

I wondered if I had been a bit impetuous in arranging this trip.

We took off at dusk, hoping to be one of the early arrivals at Annabelle and would not get caught in an airborne traffic jam where big, multiengine aircraft are flying without clearance lights.

There was no radar and no way to separate all the aircraft trying to land on a narrow road.

We flew very low, almost at wave-top level, knowing that if a Russian trawler picked us up on radar, the crew would transmit our course and speed to Nigerian defense forces. Cockpit lights were dimmed. The Nigerians had no pilots qualified to fly at night or in instrument conditions. The danger was at the destination, where a Belgian mercenary flew a bomber back and forth over Uli every night. He was called "The Intruder."

As a pilot, I knew how very difficult this flight would be and the great skill it took to find Uli Airport on a black night with no navigational signals until the very last moments of the flight.

Roland was sprawled out across the bags of salt, napping. I suspected I would get no sleep tonight and that I, too, should be napping. But I was too tense.

The pilot was a big jovial fellow from Sweden, a middle-aged guy. Like many pilots, all he wanted to do was fly. He would fly until he could no longer pass the medical exam.

He let me sit in the jump seat between him and the copilot. Below was the hammered black silver of the ocean. We swung east so not to overfly the lights of Port Harcourt. I watched the lights out a side window of the cockpit, and when I looked forward again, we were ripping across the unrelieved blackness of Nigeria. The heart of darkness. The single navigation device was a receiver for the short-range radio beacon at Annabelle. This was an ancient and primitive method of navigation. The needle flopped about, searching for something it could not find.

We had no landmarks. We had only darkness. Once the pilot picked up the radio beacon, he would overfly it on a certain heading, make a procedure turn back to the airport, and begin dropping at a standard rate of descent. If God was in His heaven, we should be on final approach. A piece of cake. Just thinking about it increased my anxiety.

The pilot looked over his shoulder and grinned and said, "You ever seen Malmo?"

"Malmo what?"

He laughed. "Malmo, Sweden, you dumb Yank."

"No, I've never been to Sweden."

"Come up there sometime. I'll show you the town. Great town."

As he talked, he adjusted the pitch of the props, pushed the throttles up a bit, and banked to enter the procedure turn. We were preparing to land. Without looking at me, the pilot said, "It might get interesting in a few minutes."

Workers on the ground heard us flying overhead and waited for a brief radio code word. Once they heard that word, they would turn on the runway lights. But for now, all the inbound aircraft were in the stygian darkness of eastern Nigeria, all maneuvering via a radio beacon to land at the same place. Now the propellers were in low pitch, the power increased, the first notch of flaps deployed. I could see the altimeter. We were below a thousand feet. The pilot picked up his microphone and whispered the code word. A band of lights came on maybe a mile in front of us.

"Once we land, the lights will go off," the pilot said. "And you will see people unload ten tons of salt quicker than you've ever seen an aircraft unloaded." His eyes locked on the runway lights, he added, "And you will move faster than you have ever moved to get your ass off this aircraft."

The flaps dropped another notch. The pilot watched the altimeter, watched the narrow runway. He was calm and relaxed. Suddenly, a giant fireball appeared in front of us; a great rushing mushroom of red and orange filled the windshield. The pilot pushed the throttles full forward and pulled back on the wheel. We flew through the top of the fireball. We disappeared into the fire. A second later, we were back in the darkness. The pilot milked up the flaps.

The pilot and copilot were tense. The copilot had his head on a swivel as he scanned the darkness. The enemy bomber had the runway zeroed in. Other cargo aircraft were lined up behind us to land. The air above Annabelle was filled with more than a dozen heavy cargo aircraft maneuvering in darkness and in radio silence. I wondered how the numerous aircraft sounded to those on the ground.

The pilot glanced over his shoulder and said, "We'll hang around an hour or so and then try again. By then, the bomber will be out of fuel or out of bombs. We should be able to get in." He shrugged, paused, and added, "Maybe."

WE landed around 1:00 a.m. As the pilot reversed the props and stood on the brakes, the aircraft shuddered and groaned. I looked out the cockpit window and saw that the runway was about ten feet wider than the landing gear. The pilot wheeled into one of the spaces cut out along the runway. Ground workers with soft flashlights guided us into an off-loading area beside the runway. The cargo door opened, and a truck backed up to the cargo door. A dozen men jumped from the truck into the aircraft and began throwing bags of salt onto a truck. From the frenzied way they worked, I knew they were not union guys.

Roland pulled at my arm. "Move. Move. We got to get away from the runway."

I looked back, waved at the pilot. "See you on the return flight," he said. His smile split the darkness. "If we are both lucky."

Another cargo aircraft, maybe a mile from the end of the runway, turned on its landing lights. The bomber was lined up again, and I saw the explosive flare of a bomb less than a half mile away. As I ducked, I felt the tremor of the bomb blast. I have never been so frightened. The aircraft landed, whirled into a revetment, and I could hear the sounds of the aircraft being unloaded.

I retrieved my small bag. Two airport workers, Biafrans in shabby clothes, barefoot, and wearing weary expressions of acceptance, were carrying Roland's case of Scotch. We ran through the low bushes. Another bomb exploded behind us. I ducked and flinched and looked over my shoulder and, in the light, I had a glimpse of the wide path we were moving along. Ahead was a small unpainted building. No lights were on anywhere, but we could see by the light of exploding bombs. Several dark figures loomed in front of me, robed figures. I slowed until Roland laughed and introduced me to two priests from the Order of the Holy Ghost. They invited us inside the one-room structure. I saw two single beds and a table.

Roland and the priests were chatting, and from the ease of their conversation, I knew they were friends. It was beginning to appear that Roland might be all he said he was. He had friends on Sao Tome and at Uli Airport.

Every few minutes, a bomb exploded, and the airport was illuminated. In the brief burst of light, I saw several airplanes in the revetments and dozens of shadowy figures moving about. I flinched and ducked with every explosion.

Roland ripped open the case of Scotch and took out two bottles, giving one to each priest. He pointed to the remaining bottles and said, "Those are for the president. I don't think he will mind that I gave two bottles to God's representatives."

Each priest held a bottle as if it were a sacred relic. I realized they had not seen a bottle of Scotch for a long time. Given that the priests were Irish, it must have seemed like an eternity. Each priest unwrapped the foil from the top of the bottle and twisted the cork.

I had expected that we would have a few drinks and the priests would stash the bottles. Instead, the priests opened the bottles and threw the corks out of the window. I stared in bewilderment. One of the priests said, "When friends come to call, we drink until it is all gone."

You have to love the Irish.

Roland and I drank away the rest of the night with two Irish priests. When the runway lights turned on, we watched and waited for the landing aircraft to come into sight, turn on its landing lights, and reach for the runway. At the moment of touchdown, both the runway lights and the aircraft landing lights turned off, and the bombs began falling. Tonight the bombers were not accurate; the bombs fell along both sides of the runway. One of the priests took a big slug of Scotch and said, "We have lost several aircraft on the ground. Each night I pray very hard for the safety of the pilots and for the safe delivery of the food aboard the airplanes." He turned and with a wry smile said, "I must admit that I find it difficult not to also pray for safe delivery of the weapons and ammunition."

Throughout the night, we watched exploding bombs and drank Scotch, and each time the runway lights came on, we saw the silhouette of a four-engine aircraft landing and other aircraft in the parking spaces along the runway. Aircraft taking off turned on their lights when they began rolling and turned them off the minute they lifted from the runway. When to take off was a roll of the dice. The pilots could not hear the bomber over the roar of their own engines. To release the brakes, turn on the landing lights, and begin the takeoff roll was an act of faith. The pilot had to believe there would not be enough time for the bomber to line up and drop a bomb on them. The forty-five seconds or so until the aircraft lifted off and doused the lights was an eternity.

That night, Roland, two priests, and I got drunk as we watched bombs bursting. Hours later, the planes stopped. We could not hear the sound of the bomber overhead, and we knew dawn was coming. And with the dawn would come Nigerian jets armed with 20-millimeter canon whose pilots would shoot at anything that moved.

"We can't drive in the morning," Roland said. He looked at one of the priests and said, "Mind if we sleep here until this afternoon?"

One of the priests held up an almost-empty bottle, smiled, and said, "You have the floor." We laughed as we stretched out on the floor, Roland with his arm locked through the handle of his gym bag.

"Where are we going tomorrow?" I asked Roland.

"Umuahia. The provisional capital. The Biafrans keep moving the capital because the Nigerians are squeezing the country tighter and tighter. Umuahia won't last much longer. In the next few months, the Biafrans will move the capital again."

I slept until midafternoon when one of the priests pointed to the small table and said, "We don't have much food. But you are welcome to share what we have."

A bowl of peanuts and a bunch of bananas was on the table.

A half hour later, Roland and I were jammed into a small car, Roland up front with the driver and me in the back with my fear. The driver ordered us to keep a sharp lookout for any aircraft. My job was to face the rear window and shout out if I saw the bomber lining up behind us on a strafing run. The driver said for me to shout if I saw the bomber. He would stop quickly, and we should run for the bush.

The ride was frightening, but we saw no aircraft. In Umuahai, Roland left me in a small featureless building called "the international press center." Roland said, "I'm staying with the president tonight. I will finalize the details of your interviews, pick you up at dawn, and take you to see the president."

I was the single reporter in the building that evening, and it was with great ceremony that I was offered dinner: a piece of gristle, a small potato, and a glass of water. The young woman who served my dinner looked at the food with great longing, and I had two thoughts: first, I realized I was eating better than 99 percent of the people in Biafra. And, second, I wondered—but did not want to know—what kind of meat I was eating.

I resolved that for the rest of my time in Biafra, I would stick with peanuts and bananas, tasty and nourishing and familiar.

The next morning, I traveled maybe ten minutes to meet the president. As I walked into the room, I saw Roland. He stood up and said, "Robert, please meet the president of Biafra, General Odumegwu Ojukwu. Mr. President, this is my friend, Robert Coram from Atlanta."

The ease with which Roland pronounced the president's name told me he had practiced often.

President Ojukwu stood up, and with a smile on his handsome face, he walked across the room, shook my hand, and said, "Welcome to Biafra." His English was clipped and precise and very British. It was the first time I had ever heard a black man speak in an English accent, and I'm sure my face showed my astonishment. In a flash of reluctant insight, I realized I was, in all the ways that were important, inferior to this man. He and I were about the same age, but he was far better educated, more poised. More worldly. It was a jarring thought. I also realized there was no small amount of irony in my coming to Africa to lose more of the racism I had grown up with in southwest Georgia.

General Ojukwu chatted easily and with confidence and was a master of facts about his country. Equally impressive was his aide, a young man named Michael Ikenzie. Michael was one of those men with an incandescent intellect. He lit up the room. I was surrounded by my betters . . . except for Roland.

"I want you to know I received the very generous donation brought here by my friend Roland," the general said. He held up the gym bag, turned to Roland and said, "Thank you again, dear friend." He handed the bag to Mike Ikenzie and said, "We will make good use of that money. My country needs everything."

Mike Ikenzie handed me a stack of brochures and documents and position papers and said, "You may wish to read these at your leisure."

I pulled out my notebook, and as I sat down to begin my interview, I could not help but wonder why the president of the country was taking time to talk with a writer from an obscure medical magazine in America. It made no sense. But as he talked, it became obvious: he was in desperate need of help from America. The more Americans who knew of his cause, the more would campaign for America to join the fray.

He, or rather Mike Ikenzie, realized that getting information about Biafra out to the world was as important—if not more important—than the food and guns being brought into Biafra.

General Ojukwu gave me great material for my story. He spoke to the medical needs of his people as well as he did to the political side of the war. His voice was pained when he said two million of his people had died from starvation. He talked of the dangers his people faced every day from Nigerian jets that roamed about shooting at anything or anyone the pilot saw. He said Uli Airport was his lifeline to the world and that without it, he would lose the war. Most of all, he talked about how many of the world powers had either lined up against him or were taking no part in the war.

He shrugged and changed the subject. "I admire your bravery in coming to Uli Airport," he said. "Not like an airport in your city of Atlanta, is it?"

An hour later, I was ready to go. General Ojukwu stood up and said, "Mike has made arrangements for you to meet with the chief doctor at Queen Elizabeth Hospital." He paused. "It is the only real hospital remaining in my country. He also made arrangements to visit a small bush hospital a few miles away. There you will see the hardships under which my people are laboring, the lack of medical supplies we face. And you will also see the heart of the Biafran people." He smiled a rueful smile and said, "You know, the English say this is not a war; it is only a tribal conflict."

I left with a feeling of fatalism about Biafra, admiration and respect for General Ojukwu, and a deep awareness that I knew little of global politics.

AT the hospital, I walked past a line of people that stretched for several hundred yards, down a long hall and ended at an open door. The people were gaunt, their eyes were haunted, and many wore bloody bandages. But it was the sight of the children that slammed me a body blow. They had the bloated bellies that, in a bit of cosmic irony, are a sign of starvation. And they had a reddish tint to their hair that is an indicator of kwashiorkor, a disease of starvation. But most of all, they had big eyes and the blank impassive stare that are signs of utter hopelessness.

The doctor was a middle-aged Englishman who was weary to the marrow of his bones. Almost a sleepwalker. He looked up from ministering to a patient when I appeared in the door. He nodded to a nurse, who walked the patient away. He forced a smile, shook my hand, and said, "You must be the writer from *Medical World News*. President Ojukwu's office called and told me to show you every courtesy." His tone made it clear he would much prefer to be with his patients than with me. But the story he gave me in a calm flat voice was horrific: the story of the effects of starvation, the horrible battlefield wounds inflicted by English-built Saladin armored cars and 20-millimeter shells from the Nigerian aircraft that roared about at low altitude.

I was shaken to the core when I walked past the long line of patients back to the waiting car. I knew I had one of the best stories of my career. And I took a solemn oath that I would never again complain about food.

That story grew better when my driver took me about thirty minutes outside Umuahia, into what he called "the bush." There a nineteen-year-old girl, after one year in medical school, was handling cases that would have challenged a doctor. The picture I took of her, stethoscope flung around her neck, clad in a shapeless off-white linen dress, her eyes old far beyond her years, would be on the cover of *Medical World News*.

Several days later, about 9:00 p.m., Roland and I took off in an empty cargo aircraft bound for Sao Tome. The second our wheels left the narrow runway, the pilot turned off the lights and banked toward the south. The flight was uneventful.

It would be ten days before I could catch a relief flight going to Europe. "It may not go to Amsterdam," Roland said. "It could go anywhere in Europe. But it is free."

I went back to Posada Salazar, a place where lizards crawled the walls and sleepy fans stirred the overheated air. Every morning, I caught a cab to the hotel and spent my day looking out over the ocean and writing my story. I spent long hours wandering alone along the beach, marveling at the coconut trees and the black sand, and thinking of all I had seen in Biafra. It was an experience that would never leave me.

AFTER stopping in New York for several days to go over my story— which would be the cover of two magazines—I flew to Atlanta. My boss was angry because I had been gone for a month, and her workload had been immense. My wife was angry because Kimberly had contracted impetigo about the time I'd left and, because this is a contagious infection, was housebound for three weeks.

But I was happy. I was a war correspondent, something that had always sounded terribly romantic. I could say I had been in Biafra, a country in Africa that would fall to the Nigerians a year later. I was changed forever.

27

I learned much about reporting from my years at the paper and at McGraw-Hill. I learned not to be intimidated by mountains of data. I learned to sort through documents, to know what is relevant, and how to distill the essence of the documents into a story. I learned how to assemble a piece while keeping an eye on the clock. And because I learned much of this in the cacophony of the city room, I could write anywhere. Put me down in the median of an interstate highway, and I can knock out a story on deadline.

I have little patience with writers who demand solitude and silence while they work, and who treat their first draft as if Moses brought it down from the mountaintop. These are the writers who wear elbow patches on tweed coats and drink tea. They do more talking than working.

This calling, this profession, this craft, this burdensome business, has been too brutal, too Darwinian, for me to indulge in such dilettante behavior.

For me, being a reporter was a postgraduate course on life. I learned the foibles and quirks, the fearsome meanness, and the uplifting nobility of my fellow man.

But there lay festering in my heart, as it does in the heart of every reporter, the desire, the dream, of writing a novel. The longer one stays at a newspaper, the greater becomes the desire. After years of writing news stories, a reporter realizes that while his work may be the first draft of history, that while he has a seat on life's fifty-yard line, his words are written in the sand. He wants to write something that will hang around for a while.

But by this time, the reporter has learned that reporting is not the same as writing. And he wonders if he stayed a reporter too long. The glory he found in being a newspaperman is now a burden on his back.

The reporter fears he may not have what it takes to write a novel. Will he get eighty or one hundred pages into the book and find he has nothing to say? Will he hit a wall and not be able to finish his book?

It's when a reporter moves on to write for a magazine, that he first begins to think of himself as a writer. So it was for me.

This is a shaky and perilous transition. Somewhere in between being a reporter and being a novelist is the middle ground of magazines: a place where reporting can lay the foundation for a story, a place where the techniques and methods of the novel can be used to give luster to the reporting. The transition is jangling and confusing and difficult.

The greatest burden is the slow-awakening knowledge that adhering to the facts can prevent one from finding the truth. This is an earth-splitting revelation, and many journalists are unwilling to abandon the ethos that made them good reporters. They find it impossible to cross the bridge and turn their backs on their beginnings.

In 1972, I went to work as one of three staff writers for *Atlanta Magazine* and began the transition from reporter to writer. At the same time, I began the transition from being a family man, a man with a wife and young daughter, a man settled into the rhythms of life to being a man who had lost his way, a man with no moral compass, a man bound for the horror of the shade.

Atlanta Magazine was still a magazine that sizzled, a magazine read far beyond the city limits, a magazine that carried the bylines of writers who would become novelists: Bill Diehl, Pat Conroy, Terry Kay, and Anne Rivers Siddons.

At *Atlanta Magazine,* I would break out of the barn and get frisky as I nibbled at the green grass that could turn a coltish reporter into a thoroughbred author. I was moving up in the caste system of writers. No longer would I be confined to the rigid formula of who-what-when-where-why. If I mastered the magazine form, perhaps one day I could write books.

For a still naive young man of thirty-five, I was one step closer to realizing a dim and hazy dream.

I had dropped out of college when I was at the *Journal.* After eight years of night classes, I was a junior. Too many times I had dropped courses because I was working on a good story. Not having a college degree in a business where a degree is the admission ticket added to my sense of inferiority. For a long time, I regretted not finishing college. And then I read that Ralph McGill never finished. He was suspended from Vanderbilt because of an article he wrote in the college newspaper. When the suspension ended, McGill was working as a newspaper reporter. He never returned to college. After that, not finishing college did not seem to matter so much.

I knew I remained a child of America's outback. I was rough and had no polish. I had no sense of style with my clothing. I often was coarse in manner and speech. I had none of the attributes often associated with writers.

But through the haze, I could still see that distant shore. Above the clanking of daily existence, I could still hear the voice that told me I could do this. I still had persistence. That the persistence came from a Southerner's defiance against the world did not matter. I had persistence.

Leslie nudged me to stay in school. But I was on the road I had always wanted to travel. And like McGill, I saw no need to go back and buy a ticket.

One story summarizes my time at *Atlanta Magazine*. The magazine then was owned by the Atlanta Chamber of Commerce, and every issue had to include a fawning profile of a local business leader or an adulatory piece about an Atlanta business. The three writers on staff referred to these stories as "suck pieces." We pushed hard against the restrictions.

I suggested a piece on the Equal Rights Amendment, then a front-page story across the country. An eloquent and fashionable woman named Phyllis Schlafly hopscotched across America, seeking to tamp down every effort to pass the ERA. I fell in with the National Organization of Women, a powerful activist group, and with the vocal support of every female on the magazine staff, convinced the managing editor and editor that publishing my story was the right thing to do. Bruce Galphin, the managing editor, came to my office door and said, "You know, this is the first advocacy piece this magazine has ever published."

The director of the chamber, a raw and basic man from west Georgia, was apoplectic when the piece came out. He was so focused on rooting out what he saw as a rebellion on staff that he paid no attention to a much bigger issue. Three women on staff had compared their salaries with the salaries of the men on staff with comparable jobs and found they were paid much less. They decided to file a complaint with the Equal Employment Opportunity Commission. I joined the complaint, which caused some befuddlement at the EEOC office. They could not understand why a man was lining up with women on the salary discrepancy issue.

The reason was simple: I had fallen in love with the graphic designer on the magazine.

Learning to unfurl my wings as a writer was not my great epiphany at the magazine. Nor was making the transition from reporter to writer. No, my great epiphany at *Atlanta Magazine* had to do with falling in love with another woman.

A married man who is having an affair thinks his great danger is in being discovered. But, no, the real danger is the risk of falling in love, falling terribly and achingly and unexpectedly in love with another woman. And with that came unimaginable agony and the need to make one of those life choices that changes things forever: stay with one's spouse, child, home, friends, and all the comfortable rhythms of life; or go with the new love, fresh love, tender love. When a fling turns into love, the emotional rocket ride scorches everything behind it. And that is what happened to me at *Atlanta Magazine*.

I will be brief in telling you of the experience. And I tell this only because I was one man when I went into the experience, and I was another altogether different man when I emerged. The experience was a hinge in my life.

The end of it all was that I resigned from *Atlanta Magazine*, divorced my wife, and left her and my daughter and ran away to Cumberland Island with the graphic designer. The first year, I was a caretaker at a large home. The second year I was a ranger for the National Park Service.

My divorce was the biggest failure in my life, and it was compounded because not only was I divorced, but also I abandoned my wife and my daughter, my child. She and my wife were left facing the shame and the cold winds of abandonment, and the scars were everlasting.

Today, my daughter is married and has two children—my grandchildren—whom I have never seen. She will not write or talk to me, and after being rebuffed many times, I understand why, and I have closed that door forever.

The wheel must be balanced. The experience I had in two years on the island had to have a counterweight. I understand that.

I learned not to talk of the two years I'd spent on the island. It is not that people don't believe me; it is that they have no frame of reference. What I experienced was a hothouse experience that can never be replicated. Those two years on the island were the most searing, intense, joyous, and painful years of my life.

But a bad beginning makes for a bad ending. My relationship with the graphic designer ended in crippling, hellish, long-lasting pain.

In the autumn of 1975, I returned to Atlanta where my younger brother, J. B. Coram, lived. He had just served a tour in the Marine Corps where he was a captain – the first officer in my family in a line that stretched back to the Revolution. He and his wife had rented a large property where they boarded horses and offered riding classes. He and his wife were approaching a divorce, and she did not want me in the house. So I lived near the horse barn in a tiny ten-by-twelve-foot plywood structure that had been a feed storage building. Rats as big as cats lived in caves under the shed. The shed was not insulated, and a cold winter was coming.

My brother's wife, another name I have forgotten, did not want me to use the single bathroom in the house, so in November and December, I got up before sunrise every morning, often the temperature was near freezing, and took the water hose for the horses' water, draped it over a fence, and turned on the faucet. I watched the arctic stream a few minutes, building courage to jump in, then I stripped and showered under the icy stream. As with a monk in the wilderness, a slow purification process began, penance for leaving my wife and daughter, a cosmic balance to my two years on the island.

After my brother's divorce, he and I rented another piece of property with a barn, and there we boarded about a dozen horses. Boarding fees paid our rent and bought our food.

While on the island, I had written a biography of Lydia Stone, a legendary woman of southeast Georgia. That book never sold. Now I was spending days and nights writing a memoir of my time on the island, a raw, visceral, cathartic book. It was the most lyrical thing I would ever write. But it, too, would never sell. In the next few years, I would write another nonfiction book and two novels, none of which ever sold. Several of those books caused New York editors to send me scathing notes telling me I was not and never would be a writer; I was beyond reclamation and should find another line of work. Those rejections and those criticisms heightened my resolve to become a writer, to prove to New York editors they did not know jack shit about who could become a writer and who could not. I continued writing, and I continued not selling my work. Had it not been for the horses' boarding fees, I would have starved.

And then one day, my world changed.

It started in such an innocuous way that it was several months before I realized I had a foundation for a new career as a freelancer. My brother was in the Marine Corps Reserves and spent weekends in a Marine aviation unit stationed at Dobbins Air Force Base north of Atlanta. Like every pilot, he had ground duties when he was not flying, and his ground job was to be the squadron intelligence officer.

One Sunday afternoon in early 1976, he told me I would never believe the number of small aircraft coming from the Bahamas into Florida without flight plans, penetrating the air defense identification zone. Most of the aircraft were suspected of carrying drugs.

He knew I would understand the significance because I had flown a small aircraft to the Bahamas and knew how important it was for every aircraft entering America from another country to be identified. An invisible offshore line formed the air defense identification zone, and a pilot entering American air space from another country could not penetrate that line without a flight plan.

I went after a story that few at the time sensed was a story. I began freelancing magazine stories about narcotics trafficking. Because I was the only person writing about drug smuggling, getting sources in law enforcement was easy. Local police, the narcotics division of the Georgia Bureau of Investigation, US Customs, and the Drug Enforcement Administration gave me extraordinary access. Once my stories began being published and law enforcement people read the stories, they began calling me. The GBI would let me know in advance if a drug bust was scheduled. US Customs allowed me to fly on their aircraft and see the airborne intercept of a drug-smuggling aircraft, the chase to America, the low-level pursuit to a Florida landing field, the high-intensity landing and ground chase, and then the arrest. I had extraordinary stories, published frequently in regional magazines.

I wondered why so many reporters were ignoring such a great story. GBI, DEA, and US Customs all said the same thing: so many reporters smoked marijuana that they had no interest in writing about narcotics smuggling, narcotics interdiction, narcotics and law enforcement, or narcotics and the effect of marijuana on young people.

In September 1978, *Esquire* published my piece about drug smuggling, the first piece in a national magazine on the topic. And it came with extraordinary details from inside Customs. It came with unprecedented photographs that a Customs officer had shot while flying over the lawless Guajira Peninsula in Colombia.

My stories gathered a lot of attention. My sources in federal law enforcement included the regional director of US Customs and the administrator of the Drug Enforcement Administration. Such sanctification enabled me to walk in and out of Customs and DEA offices in Miami, then the most important field offices in America for narcotics interdiction.

Narcotics smuggling was now on the radar of news editors. And I was considered the go-to guy for a story on any aspect of drug smuggling.

In 1979, I received the most unexpected phone call of my life: the managing editor of the *Atlanta Constitution* asked if I would bring my clips and come down and talk to him.

28

At the end of the interview, the managing editor shuffled my clips and hemmed and hawed and said he wanted to hire me, but when I was at the paper the first time, I had worked at the *Journal.* Did I want to go back to the *Journal,* or did I want to work for the *Constitution?*

Three things ran through my mind.

First, the Atlanta papers had fired me, and now, about ten years later, they wanted to hire me. Other people had left the paper voluntarily to work for other papers and then come back. But no one had been fired and then asked to come back. I would be back, and I would be the second-highest-paid reporter on the paper. I would not be on staff but would be a freelancer hired by the paper to write about drug smuggling. I would be identified as a special correspondent. It was a unique mandate. I was a hired gun. I was coming back in glory after being fired in such an ignominious fashion.

Second, I would work for the paper of McGill. He had died in 1969. But to me, this would always be the paper of McGill. I told the managing editor I wanted to work for the *Constitution.*

And third, this would be a reversal in my professional development. I was slogging away at my dream of writing books. I had gone through the intermediary step of writing for magazines and had written for most national magazines, including the *New Yorker*. And I had written five books, all rejected by New York publishers. These were not proposals, nor were they parts of manuscripts; they were full-blown four-hundred-page manuscripts. Having five books rejected by New York would cause most would-be writers to consider another line of work. But I labored on. I persisted. One day, I would be a writer.

Now, I was returning to my professional roots. I was a correspondent for the *Atlanta Constitution*.

At the paper, I had one of the most unusual jobs in American journalism. I reported to the managing editor, and I could cover any story I wanted as long as it related to drug smuggling. I would go to him and tell him I wanted to go to Colombia for several weeks and would need an expense advance. He would ask how much and would sign the approval. And off I would go. Upon my return, I turned in a story, or a series of stories, and then I would tell him I needed to go to Jamaica. He signed the approval, and off I went.

The staff did not know what to think of me. I wrote for the paper but was not on staff. I appeared to have an unlimited expense account. I was traveling to South America, the Caribbean, the Bahamas, and South Florida on a regular basis. Most of all, and based on the stories I was writing, they wondered if I was, in reality, a member of the DEA or US Customs. No reporter would write about drugs in the fashion I wrote.

I did not realize it, but sometime in the past decade, I had undergone an indefinable professional change. People I had known ten years earlier when I was at the *Journal* said that in a professional sense I had become another person, that I had moved into a zone they never expected from me. I was a different and far better reporter. I had a different way of looking at a story. My stories had depth and mass.

One day, the managing editor asked if I wanted to go on staff, to become a reporter for the *Constitution*. Of course, I said yes. At last, I would be a staff member on the paper of McGill, the job I had wanted since I was a teenager.

A year later, the paper nominated me for a Pulitzer Prize in the investigative-reporting category. I did not win, but I rejoiced in the nomination. I had come a long way from my hometown.

One of the stories on which the Pulitzer nomination rested evolved under unique circumstances. And it cemented my belief that God sometimes makes an appearance in our lives. I was still wrestling with religion. I had done as Dr. Hood had suggested when I was at Milledgeville: I believed. But I needed help with my unbelief. I still thought of myself as a sinner in the hands of an angry God. I wanted proof to support my belief. I wanted to see a pillar of cloud by day or a fire by night. I wanted to *know*.

I was about to learn that what many call coincidence or happenstance or serendipity or luck is, in reality, the subtle hand of providence. I was given my cloud by day. But I did not see it until years later when I looked over my shoulder.

This is what happened.

American law enforcement knew that many marijuana-laden aircraft coming out of the Guajira Peninsula stopped on South Caicos in the Turks and Caicos Islands. An accident of geography placed the islands halfway between Colombia and South Florida— the perfect transshipment point for narcotics traffickers. On South Caicos, the pilots refueled and spent the night and rested before the final tense dash into Florida.

The Turks and Caicos is a British Crown colony, one of the few left in the Caribbean.

The islands have a figurehead British governor, but the real power is the prime minister, who had little concern about the tons of marijuana moving through South Caicos. His lack of concern might have risen from the fact he was suspected of being on the payroll of the smugglers.

Customs and DEA agents knew what was happening on South Caicos, but they had no actionable intelligence. Plus, it would take permission from the prime minister for DEA to conduct a law enforcement operation in the Turks and Caicos. And he would not give such permission.

The DEA convinced me there was a great story on South Caicos. They suggested I fly to the island and pretend to be a pilot who wanted to get into the smuggling business. They believed that smugglers operated with such impunity and that so many local officials were in the pay of smugglers that they would welcome another potential player into the fold.

So here I was, pretending to be someone I was not in the pursuit of a story, the same thing I had been fired for at the *Journal*. You can't make this shit up.

I went to Epps Aviation in Atlanta, where I had trained for my commercial flying license, and had a long talk with the owner, Pat Epps, who said he would lend me a small single-engine Piper aircraft for a week. All I had to do was put fuel in it. But I could keep the airplane no longer than a week: Saturday to Saturday.

The time frame made me nervous. I thought it would take at least a week to dive into the underbelly of a drug-smuggling trans-shipment point and get documentation for a story. And I had to do this without being exposed as a reporter.

The managing editor did not want me to fly to South Caicos alone—a decision I agreed with—and assigned Steve Dougherty, a feature writer, to come along. I would write the hard stuff, and he would write features.

Heavy thunderstorms in Atlanta canceled our planned Saturday departure. On Sunday, the band of thunderstorms had moved to northern Florida, and again our departure was canceled. By Monday the weather system had moved offshore, and we had clear weather all the way to Fort Lauderdale.

My friend the staff member was not an early riser, and it was around 10:00 a.m. Tuesday before we took off. A little more than four hours later, we landed at Fort Lauderdale, our jumping-off point for South Caicos. Remnants of the system of thunderstorms still lingered in the southern Bahamas. That one storm system was wrecking my plans, and I grew more anxious by the day. I was not instrument qualified, and I wanted perfect weather for the final six hundred miles over water from Fort Lauderdale to South Caicos.

We took off at dawn Wednesday morning. We would land about noon and do all our research Wednesday afternoon, Thursday and Friday. Two and a half days to research a story about a major transshipment point used by dozens of drug smugglers? I had serious doubts. But the high adventure, the idea of a newspaper reporter flying a small airplane to an island dominated by drug smugglers, appealed to me. The last thing the smugglers expected was a newspaper reporter. On this island, the smugglers were safe from law enforcement.

About an hour after takeoff, we were over the Bahamas, blue sky above and blue water below. I was monitoring an air-to-air radio frequency used by pilots in the Bahamas. We droned along at 140 miles per hour, watching the different shades of water below and clouds beginning to build. My friend had never flown in a small aircraft and rubbed his hands on his legs and often turned to me to ask questions that showed his concern: What happens if the clouds build up and we can't see the ground? How do you find a small island after flying so far over the ocean? What would you do if the engine failed?

His questions were interrupted by a sudden blast of radio conversation. The person on the radio identified himself by his aircraft numbers and said, "Hey, hey, hey, anybody out there listening?"

I shook my head in disbelief at the pilot's lack of professionalism and did not answer his call. After a moment he came back. "Hey, hey, hey, anybody out there listening?"

This time I picked up the microphone, gave him my aircraft number, and asked if he was having an inflight problem.

He laughed and said he sure as hell was. He had been in Miami partying all night, and now he and three friends were headed to South Caicos. His three friends were passed out, and he was exhausted. He wanted someone to talk to. He wanted someone to keep him awake until he got to South Caicos. He could not motor along, looking at the endless sky and the endless sea, listening to the drone of the engine without falling asleep. "Talk about anything," he said. "Just talk to me."

I told him we were also going to South Caicos. As we talked, we discovered we were staying at the same hotel. When he asked why I was going to South Caicos, I used the coded and coy language of drug smugglers to say I was thinking of going "down south" and might be "bringing some cargo back," and I was just checking out a possible refueling point for the return trip.

His knowing laugh told me he knew what I was talking about. As he began his descent for landing, he thanked me for keeping him awake for several hours. "Man, you saved my life," he said. "I wouldn't have made it without you. I owe you."

And then straight ahead was South Caicos. My talkative radio friend was waiting when we landed, standing beside his aircraft with a big grin on his face. He was medium height and a bit on the pudgy side.

After introductions, he said lunch was on him. I told him I had to first clear Customs and Immigration and get a car and check into the hotel and would be delighted to have lunch.

He said, "Forget about Customs and Immigration. Forget about a car." He would take us anywhere we wanted to go. He turned and waved to a Customs officer and to an immigration officer, indicated that we were with him, and off we went along the winding road into Cockburn Harbour. There was one hotel on the island, the Admiral's Arms, and that is where we went.

It turned out that my radio friend was the chief pilot for the largest group of smugglers operating out of South Caicos. His power on the island was immense. After lunch, he drove us back to the airport and introduced us to the tower chief, who told us the proper radio frequencies to use when we were inbound with cargo. He told us how much it would cost to bring cargo through his airport. Customs and Immigration told us the fee for immunity when coming through with a load. These conversations were straightforward and businesslike.

At dinner that evening, Steve, the feature writer, and I walked into a dining room and found two large tables. One table was occupied by fishermen and divers, identified by big watches, tanned complexions, and casual clothing. The smugglers were identified by their cowboy boots, pressed jeans, and stylish shirts. We sat with the smugglers.

After dinner, the smugglers leaned back, lit up joints, and began telling stories about the Guajira, about eluding Customs aircraft, about dangerous night landings in a Florida pasture. Steve joined them in smoking pot, which increased our credibility with these gentlemen. I did not smoke and got away with it because I said pot caused me to have nightmares.

After dinner, Steve and I went to our room, pulled our notebooks from under our mattresses, and scribbled for hours, reaching into our memory banks to recall conversations and radio frequencies and landing procedures. I told Steve I had almost everything I needed. Because of our pilot friend, we had met everyone on the island who was important to a drug trafficker. What I thought would take four or five days, I had done in one afternoon. We would hang around until noon tomorrow so Steve could gather material for a feature story and then fly a short hop to Grand Turk, where I would call the governor. Friday, we would get up at dawn, fly to Fort Lauderdale, refuel, and strike out for Atlanta. It would be a very long day.

The governor was a young British civil servant, lean, intense, and earnest. He was on his first assignment with the Foreign Office and was so flattered that a reporter from an American newspaper would call that he invited us down at our convenience. Not only did he know about the drug smugglers on South Caicos, but he also volunteered that the smuggling business was "a bloody great wart on the end of our nose."

I loved this guy.

My story took up half the front page of the Sunday paper. It was reprinted in numerous American newspapers, all across Great Britain, and in Europe. It was a sensation. An intelligence officer for US Customs called from Fort Lauderdale to say the story was the best intelligence document he had ever read. He could not believe I had the radio frequencies used by smugglers and the amount of money it would cost to bring a load through South Caicos. The British government was so embarrassed by the story it sent a narcotics enforcement officer from London to Grand Turk. The British also sent two RAF pilots to patrol the islands with the narcotics officer. A British TV network flew a crew to America to interview me and later did a documentary based on my story. Several Miami television stations interviewed me at my desk in Atlanta.

Backlash from American smugglers was quick. My vanity caused me to be snookered by several people connected to drug smugglers.

The most embarrassing was when a prominent lawyer called and said he had a client who wanted to build a marina on Grand Turk. The client did not know where to place the marina and wanted my advice. What the hell do I know about where to put a marina? But the lawyer was importunate. I went to his house in a wealthy part of Atlanta. He and I sat on a sofa. He opened a map, and I looked around and said, "What do you think of this spot?"

When I sat down, I was facing a closet door across the room. The door had louvers on the front. As I talked to the lawyer, I heard a camera clicking and realized someone behind the door was taking pictures. After about two minutes, the lawyer said he thought that was enough, folded the map, and stood up to escort me to the door. I realized he thought I was a not-so-bright newspaper reporter. And perhaps I was.

A few weeks later, undercover DEA and Customs officers who worked the Caribbean called to tell me my picture was tacked up behind the door of restaurants and bars throughout the region, from the Bahamas through the Turks and Caicos and Jamaica. "These guys are looking for you," they said. "You shouldn't go down there for a while."

When I thought of my trip and connected the dots, I realized that none of the events was coincidence or happenstance or fortuitous. Being delayed by thunderstorms for three days was not the disaster I thought. Because of the delay, I was in the air at the same time as the smuggling pilot, going to the same island, staying at the same hotel. Had I gone to South Caicos on schedule, I would never in a thousand years have been able to talk with the officials on South Caicos who made things happen. This was a story I was meant to write. This was my story.

IN the late 1970s and into the 1980s, much of the marijuana being smuggled into America came through South Florida. The reason was simple: airplanes loaded with marijuana have a limited range. Many of the smugglers took off from Colombia, refueled in the Turks and Caicos Islands, and then took off for South Florida— some six hundred miles away and at the very end of their range. South Florida was their first stop. And they liked the rural and open and farming side of southwest Florida. One of my best sources was Ralph Cunningham, the chief investigator for the state's attorney who represented five counties in deep southwest Florida. He often went undercover and worked with smugglers. I did several stories that portrayed him as a crusading law enforcement officer and, perhaps even more important, portrayed his boss as a hard-nosed prosecutor. His boss told my source to keep talking to me.

Ralph was short and fat and talked like a redneck boob. And that made him a great undercover officer. Many smugglers hired him as an off-loader or as a guard at a landing site and found out later in court that he had an encyclopedic knowledge of their operation. They were hauled off to jail still not understanding how the dumb little fat man had outwitted them.

One day Ralph mentioned that a Senate investigative committee was looking into the finances of drug smuggling. They wanted to know how much money was involved in the business, how much money was being laundered in Florida. Senate staffers in Washington knew nothing of South Florida, the quantity of drugs cascading through there, who was paid off, and how much money was involved. They looked around and thought my friend, the chief investigator, knew more than anyone else, and they asked him to put together a wide-ranging report. They would use his data as the foundation for the Senate report.

The chief investigator told me he had almost completed the report.

By this time, I had written narcotics smuggling articles for a dozen or so magazines, including the Sunday magazine of the *St. Petersburg Times*. On this day, the editor of the magazine was driving me to the airport for a return flight to Atlanta and mentioned in passing that she had been thinking about a story on the financial side of drug smuggling. She had an idea that unimaginable amounts of money were involved.

I turned to her and said, "I have that story." She commissioned me on the spot to write what she said would be a cover story.

I called the chief investigator who said, of course, he would send me a draft copy of his report. It was almost ready to send to the Senate staffers.

The report laid bare the intricate and layered complexity of the narcotics money trail, the most fascinating part of which was the complicity of banks in South Florida in accepting hundreds of millions of dollars in drug money and taking 2 percent as a fee, a fee that reached millions of dollars.

My story in the *St. Petersburg Times* magazine created a firestorm of indignation. Most people had no idea that drug smuggling generated such large sums and that respectable banks were so complicit in helping smugglers launder their money. And a month or so later, when the Senate committee, with much fanfare, published its investigation into the money involved in drug smuggling, they also got many comments. But the comments were not congratulatory. Instead, the questioners wanted to know why they had copied the story in the *St. Petersburg Times*.

I dwell on this narcotics business for several reasons. First, it was my stories that first brought narcotics trafficking and its consequences to public attention.

I began writing of smuggling in the mid-1970s when it was marijuana trafficking. The smugglers were good old boys, and when caught, they would throw up their hands, say, "Guess you caught me speeding," and then go away for a few months in jail. Few smugglers carried weapons. It was not a violent business. But the business changed in the 1980s when Colombians became involved. They smuggled cocaine, carried automatic weapons, and were not afraid to use them. The advent of the violent cocaine cowboys was a pivotal moment in the smuggling business. When cocaine and guns became part of the mix, I knew it was time for me to get out.

By now, narcotics trafficking was a national story. I owned the story. I was getting out at the apex of my newspaper reporting career. Then along came a story I could not turn down. I had one more story I wanted to write.

29

My last story about drug smuggling was another bit of what many would call "cowboy journalism." I preferred to call it "initiative reporting" or "shoe-leather reporting." Call it what you will. I was having the time of my life.

The story was about Bimini, a little Bahamian sand bar about fifty miles east of Fort Lauderdale. And once again, what many would call coincidence played a big part in the story.

Nick Navarro, the sheriff of Broward County in South Florida, knew my work. He was married to a woman whose family lived in Atlanta. Sheriff Navarro wanted to use me to increase his standing with his mother-in-law. A story in his in-law's hometown newspaper about his department's Bahamian undercover operations would do just fine. His was an agenda that served my needs.

A sheriff's jurisdiction ends at the country line. He certainly has no jurisdiction in a foreign country. Conducting a law enforcement operation in a foreign country is defined as espionage. But this was 1980, and if the sheriff of Broward County wanted to impress his in-laws, there were no rules.

A confidential informant told the sheriff that a big drug operation was about to go down on Bimini and the sheriff wanted to bust it.

If I was interested in the story, he would put me in the middle of what he called "Operation Limey."

The sheriff reminded me that my photo was on the wall in many Bahamian bars and marinas, and suggested I change my appearance. He thought I might lighten my hair and let it grow, have a permanent to make it frizzy, and wear a half-dozen gold chains around my neck. I should talk louder and adopt a more aggressive persona. I would be posing as a drug smuggler, and many drug smugglers have hair-trigger tempers. I was to become a real badass with a very short fuse. I would be aboard a boat and should study navigation charts of Bimini and the surrounding waters. I had to know the shallow and treacherous waters of Bimini, the reefs and sandbars, as well as a smuggler.

The undercover agent was a mischievous young deputy sheriff named Nigel Fullick, who thought I was too old to accompany him. But the sheriff was adamant. "You will take him with you," he ordered.

Nigel drove me to where he'd hidden a boat that had been confiscated from smugglers. It was a yellow cigarette boat, a sleek thirty-foot craft with two outboard engines on the stern. Nigel stashed two pistols in a hidden part of the cockpit and told me might have to use the guns before this trip was over. I said I was a reporter, not a police officer, and that I could not use a gun. He looked at me with a combination of disgust and disbelief.

As we rumbled out of Fort Lauderdale, we passed the US Customs station. I asked if we should file departure forms. Nigel said we were not officially leaving Broward County, so there was no need to fill out paperwork.

It was dark when we idled up to the long channel that leads to the dock in front of the Big Game Club on Bimini. We passed a cabin boat of forty-two-feet. Nigel leaned over and checked the stern of the yacht so he could read the name. "That's the boat carrying the dope," he said. He shook his head when he looked at the three outboard engines on the stern. "His engines are bigger than ours, and the boat is faster," he said. His tone told me that was not a good thing.

Two rough men lounged on the rear deck, and their eyes never left us as we idled past and docked maybe thirty feet in front of them. We tied our boat to the dock, then sat in the dark not talking. We were sitting below dock level in the dark. But dock lights illuminated the boat behind us.

About an hour later, a go-fast boat showing no lights eased up alongside the cabin boat. We heard the grunts of men as they passed large boxes from the yacht to the smaller vessel and the thump as those boxes hit the deck. We watched the laden craft ease away from the dock and rumble down the long channel before reaching deep water and turning west. We saw the boat settle by the stern then leap up on plane as the boat accelerated and then the sound of powerful engines. In the moonlight, we saw the wide white wake and followed the course of the boat.

"He's not going due west," Nigel mumbled, "maybe two-sixty. My guess is he is going to Homestead. You stay here." Laughing aloud, as if he had been drinking, he crawled out of the boat and lurched toward the lights of the Big Game Club. He stumbled and mumbled, and I could hear, "I need another Bahama Mama." From the darkness, I saw two men on the yacht watching him.

Five minutes later, Nigel returned, still playing the happy drunk. As he lurched into the boat, he whispered that Customs was waiting for the doper boat. They would get popped offshore. He had called the Broward sheriff, reported what he'd seen, and the sheriff had relayed the information to the Customs command post.

Another go-fast boat idled up against the yacht. We heard a quick exchange of conversation and again the bumps and thunks and heavy breathing. Soon, the boat, noticeably lower in the water, idled away from the dock and down the channel, the powerful rumble of its engines murmuring across the water.

Nigel watched as the boat turned west and accelerated. "I'm guessing Palm Beach," he said. Again, he crawled out of the boat, and in a loud voice said, "I have to piss," and lurched toward the Big Game Club.

This happened again before I noticed men in the yacht down standing on the forward deck and studying us in the darkness. They could see only a shadowy outline. Their eyes never left Nigel as he ambled toward the bar.

As he returned to our boat, another go-fast boat tied up to the cabin boat. We heard a squeak when the boat slid off the fenders on the cabin boat.

Nigel watched the departure, glanced toward the yacht, and said, "As soon as I make this call, we are hauling ass. They are getting suspicious." He pulled out one of the hidden guns, an enormous nickel-plated revolver, a .44 Magnum, handed it to me, and said, "Don't be afraid to use this." He walked away. One of the men jumped on the dock and began following him.

At the same time, another man from the yacht jumped to the dock and walked toward us. I knew he was going to get into the boat. I could see him, but he could not see me. He stopped on the dock overhead, and as he crouched to step into our boat, I banged the revolver against the chrome sissy bar and cleared my throat.

The man froze, paused a moment, then turned and walked toward the yacht.

When Nigel returned, I was panicky. "They tried to board while you were gone."

"Yeah, I know," he said, voice tight. "The other guy saw me on the phone. I think they have snapped to us. We got to get out of Dodge."

It was a little after 1:00 a.m.

We cast off, and Nigel nudged the throttles. I looked at him in astonishment. We were not going forward but rather pushing stern first toward the dope boat. Nigel swung the stern out to clear the bow of the yacht, then moved down alongside the boat. We could have reached out and touched the boat. The three hard men on stern were nonplussed to see us so close. Then Nigel thrust the throttles forward, the boat squatted, and we wheeled and threw a big bow wave against the other boat, rocking it, causing it to compress the rubber fenders and bang against the dock. We heard cursing, then urgent commands, and saw the crew untying the boat from the dock. Nigel pushed the throttles all the way forward, and the boat squatted and raced away from the dock at a speed that would bring censure from the dock master.

We were several hundred yards down the channel when we saw the cabin boat roaring after us, bow high as it gathered speed and a white V broadening behind it. "Nigel, they are chasing us," I said in my high voice.

He said, "Yeah, I hope they can't catch us. Hold on."

The length of South Bimini passed close on our port side. Hearing what sounded like mosquitoes buzzing overhead, I looked over my shoulder and saw dots of red lights. "Nigel, what are those red lights?"

He ducked, said, "Damn, they are shooting at us," and began zigzagging the boat. He shouted for me to jump overboard and swim to shore. I grabbed the sissy bar and moved as far away from him as I could.

"You are out of your mind," I said. "These are the most shark-infested waters on the planet."

"I get paid for this!" he shouted. "You don't. Get overboard."

I clung to the sissy bar. No way in hell was I going overboard.

I think he would have thrown me overboard, but he had more pressing problems. The other boat was gaining on us. Nigel kept snapping his head over his shoulder and then ahead. He grinned a fiendish grin and said, "Let's see how big their balls are." As we passed the southern end of the island, he swung hard left. We were in Nixon Bay, a wide curving bay on the southeast corner of South Bimini. According to marine charts, these are not navigable waters. The water was clear, and I could see the sandy bottom and knew we were clearing the bottom by inches. Clouds of sand boiled behind us. We were approaching the beach at high speed. Then Nigel swung the wheel hard again, and we were in deep water. He chopped the throttles, and we sat there, breathing hard as the boat slowed, then stopped.

The boat pursuing us did not come into Nixon Bay. At the spot where we'd turned left, they stopped. We could see them a half mile away, as they rocked in the swells, waiting.

Nigel pointed to the shore where an enormous house built on pilings stood dark in the night. "A doper built that," he said. "He dug out this little place where he is going to build a dock. He is going to cut a channel out to deep water. I don't know what he is waiting for. But I'm glad he hasn't dug the channel."

He looked around. "The tide is rising. In a couple of hours, they may get up the nerve to come in here. Until then, they will wait us out. If they don't leave soon, we go to plan B."

"What is plan B?" I asked.

He smiled a rakish pirate smile.

An hour later, he murmured, "Here we go." He cranked up the big engines, and we backed across the dark water until we were at the very edge of the shallow water and almost on the beach. Nigel looked at me and said, "Hold on. Hope this works."

He shoved the throttles forward, and we were on the plane before we hit the shallow flats. Again, I could see the sandy bottom and the plumes of sand kicking up in our wake. Nigel swung the wheel hard to the right, and we were aimed at the mountains of large rocks strung along the western edge of the island, extending south into deep water.

"You can't get through there!" I shouted. I was holding the sissy bar so tight I almost ripped it out.

Nigel bent over the wheel, tense, guiding the boat toward the rocks. I hunkered down, believing we were about to go up in a ball of flames. I could have reached out and touched the large rough-edged rocks on either side of the boat. Just a scrape and the bottom would be ripped out of our boat.

We broke through into open water, and Nigel let out an exultant shout. I realized he had used the extra foot or eighteen inches of water that came with the high tide to cut through a gap in the rocks.

We looked over our shoulders, and in the moonlight, we saw white water fan out from the wake of the doper boat and knew they were again in pursuit.

A few seconds later, Nigel swung the boat right, and we entered the narrow Mackle Cut, a canal dug by a developer years earlier. Thick mangrove bushes lined the banks. We swung left to follow the canal, and Nigel slowed as he rammed the boat into a mangrove thicket. I ducked as the branches lashed the sides of the boat and whipped over my head. Nigel cut the engines and said, "I hope to hell we are far enough in the bushes that they can't see us." He retrieved his guns from the side panel, handed me the revolver, and said, "If they stop, that means they have seen us. We shoot first."

I had no time to answer. The smugglers' boat was entering the cut. The skipper guided the boat as his two companions lined the stern, both holding automatic rifles at the ready. The boat chugged past us, engines rumbling, a boiling wake behind the boat. The smugglers looked hard at the mangrove bushes on either side of the channel. Their bodies tense, their weapons at the ready.

They passed, and Nigel whispered, "They can't see us. We'll sit here until daylight. They don't know if we went out the other end of the canal or if we are in here. They will be back."

The first hint of dawn was breaking to the east as the smugglers made their last pass in front of us, frustration evident in their tense bodies. As their boat disappeared toward the west, Nigel stood up, laughed, and said, "Bet you don't do this every day, reporter man."

A half hour later, we roared out of the cut bound for Fort Lauderdale. We crossed the Gulf Stream, and as we drifted past the Customs station, I asked if we were going to stop and do the paperwork. Nigel laughed. "We never left. So why should we sign in?"

Two days later, he called me in Atlanta and said the feds had confiscated the four boats we had watched leave Bimini. The feds had seized the dope and arrested every crew member. As always, the feds took the credit. Sheriff Navarro didn't care. His in-laws had read my story.

That story caused the Bahamian government to complain to the State Department about Sheriff Navarro. The Bahamian government declared me *persona non grata*.

The closeness with which we avoided being shot rattled me. Nigel was right. I don't do this every day. It was time for me to retire from the dope-smuggling business.

30

CUMBERLAND Island, the island where I had lived for two years, the island that was the hinge of my life, was in the news. The National Park Service had published its management plan for the island. The plan would guide the park service for the foreseeable future.

The NPS wanted to use a bigger boat to take visitors to the island. Build commercial fast-food outlets. A tram to run up and down through the wilderness area. The NPS began holding public hearings, and the first was so contentious that I sensed a great anger from the general public. The public wanted the park service to forget the management plan and do nothing; the public wanted the NPS to leave the island in its natural state. Because I had lived on the island for two years, I had an intense personal interest in the issue. I told myself that I was using the expertise I had gained as a house sitter on the island and then a year as a ranger with the NPS. I knew both sides of this argument as well as anyone. But it was personal. My time on the island was hidden in a back corner of my heart. But now it jumped to the forefront, and I was going to make this story mine. I was going to make sure my island, *my island*, remained as I remembered it, as I would always remember it.

I asked the managing editor if I could devote full time to covering what I saw was the coming battle. He had nominated me for a Pulitzer Prize in investigative reporting for my narcotics trafficking stories. Again, he turned me loose. My romantic side, my anal nature, my sense of indignation—every facet of my being came into action on this story. The NPS would not pour any pills down the toilet, not on my watch.

For months, I covered every NPS hearing. I sought interviews with conservation groups, environmental groups, island visitors. I interviewed anyone with an opinion and some who did not know they had an opinion until I told them they did. The editors sensed this could be a story with wide public interest and put most of my stories on the front page. The park service was overwhelmed by the public response. More than three thousand people wrote letters to the park service, and they all said the same thing: Keep your grubby hands off the island. Let it stay wild.

The regional director of the park service was bewildered. He told me that the park service did not get three thousand letters over issues in Yosemite or Yellowstone. Cumberland Island National Seashore was a new and obscure park off the Georgia coast. It was a park many people did not know existed. The passionate opposition to the management plan made no sense. Not to the park service.

Nine months after making the plan public, the park service threw it out. The island would remain in its wild state.

That series of articles resulted in another Pulitzer nomination, this one in the public service category, the most prestigious category. Again, I did not win. But the nomination was a matter of pride. The environmental groups who favored the plan, the NPS, and local people in the coastal county where the island was located knew this issue was personal with me. They fumed and griped, but in the end, they capitulated.

A few weeks after the NPS dropped the management plan, I was at my desk when I sensed a looming presence. I looked up, and there stood Jim Minter, the editor of the paper. He was a most intimidating presence. I sensed that the eyes of everyone in the newsroom had followed Minter across the room. He was a quiet and soft-spoken man, stern-faced, a man who was all business. For an editor, he was a man of few words. "I want you to go to El Salvador," he said. "Cover the election down there. After that, go anywhere you want to in Central America. Just send me good stories."

And then he was gone. I stared after him, my mouth hanging open. El Salvador? They are having a war down there. I've had my war. I don't need a war in Central America.

I sat stunned for a few minutes. I noticed the managing editor was staring through the walls of his glass office toward me. He raised his hands as if to say, what the hell was that all about?

I walked across the city room into his office and said, "Jim Minter wants me to cover the election in El Salvador." It was clear that the managing editor had not known of this plan. He was as surprised as I was. He shook his head and said, "Figure out how much money you need and get ready to go. When is the election?"

"I don't know. I just know that Jim Minter said they are about to have an election."

A few days later, I landed in San Salvador, the capital of El Salvador. The election supervisor was a doctor, an OBGYN. I was interviewing him in his office in a hospital on the outskirts of town when rebels attacked. Bullets shattered windows, and the snap of rifle fire was loud. Why the hell would anyone attack a hospital? The doctor and I huddled under his desk and continued talking. He compared the coming election to the birth process: painful, much blood. Sometimes requires emergency procedures. But in the end, a new life comes into the world.

My stories from El Salvador were all on the front page. But the interview with the doctor was above the fold and stripped across the top of the paper.

A week after I returned from El Salvador, Jim Stewart, the new assistant managing editor for news, called me to his office and fired me. He said my interviewing techniques were too aggressive. I asked him for an example, but he would give me none.

I challenged him and said he did not have the authority to fire me. He said he had taken the new job on the condition that he could hire and fire. When I came out of his office, the city editor and assistant city editors were staring. They had *that* look on their faces. They knew. And by the time I cleaned out my desk, everyone in the city room knew.

I had been on staff for two years, been nominated for a Pulitzer each year, chosen by the editor to cover a war, and had more than three hundred bylines, as many on the front page as any reporter at the paper. And the first official act of the new assistant managing editor was to fire me.

Now I had been fired from both the *Journal* and the *Constitution*. A few months later, the two papers merged, and I knew my record of being fired from both papers could never again be replicated. I had done something unique.

Except for the job at McGraw-Hill, I had failed at every job I ever had: North Georgia College, the air force, Milledgeville, three jobs in Atlanta before going to work for the *Journal*, the *Journal*, *Atlanta Magazine*, and now the *Constitution*. And there was no way I could rationalize this and turn the blame on my employers. It was virtually unanimous: I was not a good employee.

This time there was no weeping and wailing about being fired. The next day, I was working on freelance magazine pieces and picking up speed on another book. I had an unblemished record of failure with my previous five books, but I sensed—I *hoped*—I was learning more about writing, about this perilous and heartbreaking business of writing.

I went back to my roots and concentrated on nonfiction disguised as novels. While I was writing about narcotics trafficking, I had run across numerous stories that would not work in a newspaper. One of those stories became a book about cops and smugglers. In 1988, I sold *Narcs*. It was a mass-market paperback sale, and I was paid only a few thousand dollars. But I had sold my first book. That book became the first in a series of three books about drug smuggling. Then came four police procedurals based in Atlanta. I had written seven novels, all mass-market paperbacks, and people had stayed away in droves. But I continued to write. And I continued to learn.

Then came a hodgepodge of nonfiction books, a collaboration with an Irish woman who went to Vietnam to work with street children, a fishing book for *National Geographic*, and an investigative book about US complicity in the corruption of Antigua. Years later, *Bridge Across My Sorrows*, the book with the Irish woman, would become a movie titled *Noble*. But the other books disappeared.

In 1998, I looked back at those ten books and realized my career was at a crossroads. My books were mediocre and remembered only for the speed at which they were remaindered. I had run out of ideas and did not know what was next. Mel Berger, my agent at William Morris, was thinking about dropping me.

Out of desperation, I called a friend in Washington, DC, who, for more than a decade, had been pushing me to write a biography of his hero and mentor, air force retired Colonel John Boyd. I went to Washington and after a few days of interviews, realized this would be a complex book, a big book. My agent sent out several dozen copies of my book proposal, and within hours, Little, Brown and Company, one of the most venerated houses in America, made an offer.

Four years later, *Boyd* was published. More than forty reviews came in, reviews from as far away as Australia. The *New York Times* reviewed the book, as did the *Washington Post*. Sales reached more than a hundred thousand copies, and today, fifteen years later, the book continues to sell. Little, Brown liked *Boyd* so much they offered me a two-book contract that stipulated that both books would be military biographies. Both additional books, *American Patriot* and *Brute,* were reviewed in national newspapers.

Writing military biographies was not part of my career plan. But no writer turns down a two-book contract from Little, Brown. Thus, I became a military biographer. After the Little, Brown contract expired, I wrote another military biography for St. Martin's Press.

Several reviewers said I was the best military biographer in America. That is a grandiose statement, and I am not sure I agree. But who am I to argue with such distinguished critics?

That I, who had been kicked out of the air force, wrote military biographies is the ultimate irony. And it shows that God has a wicked sense of humor.

My military books became iconic within the military, were taught at the service academies, and two were on the Commandant of the Marine Corps' reading list. If I am remembered as a writer, it will be for my military biographies, especially for the Boyd bio.

The thread woven through almost every review of my biographies is that they are well researched. The strength of my work is the reporting, not the writing. I am pleased by that, but I also feel I never reached my goal. I wanted to be an elegant writer. But I am not. There is nothing elegant about me. But I can live with being considered a good reporter.

And, while it is self-serving to say so, I have come to believe that biography is the highest form of nonfiction writing. I say that because it is men and women who make history, and the narrative stream of a biography is the best way to reveal the "who" and the "why" and the "how" of history.

Military biographies brought my life full circle. After I was tossed out of the air force, I stayed away from anything to do with the military. Fifty years later, I was writing books that make me, at last, understand my father, respect him for his service to his country, and love him for the qualities and ideals he represented.

My epiphany came about when I was writing *American Patriot*, the biography of air force colonel Bud Day. Colonel Day was shot down in Vietnam and would spend six years in the infamous Hanoi Hilton. He was tortured almost to the point of death. All he had to do to stop the torture was to sign a piece of paper saying he thought the war in Vietnam was immoral. The attorney general, prominent senators, and half the college students in America said the war was immoral. But Bud Day did not have that freedom. He was a serving officer in time of war and in the hands of the enemy. He would die before he gave more than his name, rank, and date of birth. In holding fast, he exemplified the patriotism, sense of duty, courage, and willingness to die for his beliefs that represent the American military. When Colonel Day told me this story, I realized that he personified the beliefs my daddy had tried to teach me when I was a boy, teachings that I rejected. I realized that in some odd and twisted way, my daddy made me who I am.

I have scattered many words across the landscape and had a better run than most. Today, after publishing fifteen books, I am coasting, enjoying what Oliver Wendell Holmes called the final canter after crossing the finish line. I often think of the line from Sophocles: "One must wait until the evening to know how splendid the day has been." And I have had a splendid day; I have come farther from my roots than I ever thought I would. I have accomplished most of what I hoped I would ever accomplish. I have come farther than many of my contemporaries, most of whom are better writers than am I.

The writing life has been a good life, and I continue to write. But now it is from habit and not from purpose. I must feed the beast.

For a long time, I dwelled on my failures. But now I can look back and see how each failure laid the foundation for what followed.

Today, everything about being a newspaperman has changed. The *Atlanta Journal-Constitution* is no longer recognized nationally. The paper has no one on staff who has an institutional knowledge of Georgia politics, Georgia business, or statewide issues. There is no crusading and feared investigative reporter. The paper's low-calorie journalism makes it at best a regional paper. Most painful of all, at least to me, is that many of the "content providers"—they are not called reporters—have moved into the newsrooms of their local television affiliate. My God, reporters working in a television newsroom. We are jangled indeed when the paper quotes the TV station, and the TV station quotes the newspaper. What I, in my ancient frame of reference, regard as sleeping with the enemy, now is seen as progress, a way to rescue a newspaper.

There is no McGill, Pennington, or Nelson on staff. There is no one at the paper who is quoted on a regular basis by the national media. There is no conscience of the South. There is no voice that soars to a national level and no reporting that brings glory to the paper. Local television drives the news agenda. Local television breaks most of the big stories. Local television *owns* most of the big stories. And it seems every other television reporter is described on-air as an "investigative reporter," a once-revered title that today is passed around like a party favor.

In this new world, social media has become the primary source of news. Social media? I am not sure what "social media" means. But it gives voice to people who have never been heard and who have nothing to say. Much of social media is mean and dark, and every posting threatens more than two hundred years of journalism tradition. There has never been more information available than there is today. But much of it is unreliable, word-of-mouth gossip. Bad information is ubiquitous; good information is rare and is for the few remaining traditionalists. The inmates are in charge, and everyone is a reporter.

The world has passed me by.

But I was fortunate to be a reporter for a major metropolitan daily at a time when that daily was respected across America. I worked for a newspaper whose reporters were giants striding across the earth. I worked for the Atlanta newspapers when facts were sacred, when print journalism was at high tide and when Atlanta was becoming Atlanta and when America was in turmoil. I covered the civil rights movement, the most important story of my time. I was a newspaperman when it meant something to be a newspaperman. I had the greatest title a young man could have: reporter.

Today when I sit nodding in front of my fire and thinking of days gone by, it is not my books that I think of but rather my days as a newspaperman. It is the music of the presses I hear, the snarling of the news beast that I feel, the pages of newsprint that I see, and the hustle of the city room that I remember. Being young and a reporter was the great experience of my life. I come back to the beginning, and it is all new.

CPSIA information can be obtained
at www.ICGtesting.com
Printed in the USA
LVHW091255120419
613974LV00001B/67/P